Mustang

The Original Pony Car 1964-2011

Published by

Krause Publications, a division of F+W Media, Inc.
700 East State Street • Iola, WI 54990-0001
715-445-2214 • 888-457-2873
www.krausebooks.com

To order books or other products call toll-free 1-800-258-0929
or visit us online at www.krausebooks.com or www.Shop.Collect.com

Library of Congress Control Number: 2010931154

ISBN-13: 978-1-4402-1548-3
ISBN-10: 1-4402-1548-0

Designed by Sharon Bartsch
Edited by Brian Earnest

Printed in the United States of America

CONTENTS

FOREWORD...*4*

1960..*5*

1970.. *43*

1980.. *66*

1990 .... *108*

2000... *166*

EVERYONE LOVES A PONY

The fabulous Mustang has successfully survived and adapted to America's market changes, political climate swings, gas shortages and shifts in corporate direction at Ford Motor Company for more than four decades.

When introduced in April 1964, young couples and small middle class families were hungry for a stylish, medium-size offering that could be built to accommodate any budget with a range of six-cylinder and V-8 engines. The new Mustang became as much an overnight sensation as The Beatles had just two months earlier on their first visit to America.

When its competition finally arrived from Chevrolet, Pontiac, AMC and the entire MOPAR family in 1967, Ford cranked up the Mustang's output with a 390- and later 428-cid big-block V-8. By 1969, fighting the escalating performance wars pumped the Mustang into a bulky but sleek racer for the street, strip or road course when the stable was filled with such thoroughbreds as the Boss 302, Boss 429, Shelby GT-350, Shelby GT-500 and Mach 1.

Unfortunately, all of the other car companies had just as many individual performance models vying for market share. The proliferation of high-horsepower pony and muscle cars, combined with stricter federal regulations and growing insurance premiums, led to the demise of the segment. In 1971, the Mustang had a bloated body and only a few engines to give it any real motivation.

Ford went in the opposite direction in 1974 by bringing to market a Mustang smaller than the original and "powered" by a pair of sub-par engines. Emasculating the once-proud pony would surely have killed off the marque had the Mustang II's introduction not coincided with the Organization of Petroleum Exporting Countries' (OPEC) year-long oil embargo against the United States and other supporters of Israel. Turning the Mustang into what passed at the time for an economy sub-compact wound up being its salvation when 1974 sales nearly tripled the numbers from 1973.

As foreign car manufacturers — especially those from the Pacific Rim — gobbled up pieces of the American car market during the '70s, Ford was preparing a third-generation Mustang with European flair, Japanese build quality and red-white-and-blue sex appeal. Known as the "Fox" Mustang by Ford insiders and fans, the 1979 through 1993 model originally served as a test bed for the company's forward-looking (though doomed) turbocharger technology but would resurrect the car's performance image when later coupled with the popular 5.0-liter V-8.

So advanced was the Fox platform that even a major re-design in 1994 carried over several primary chassis components. The most aerodynamic Mustang to date still managed to incorporate several styling cues from the marque's history including the horse corral on the grille, three-element taillamps and side scoops. A 1999 facelift took the look even further into retro territory with a more muscular body and exaggerated fake air intakes.

Once it was clear the Mustang had outlived all of its competition (the Camaro/Firebird being the last to go), Ford introduced its 2005 model—a car so similar in appearance and size to the 1960s original that some shoppers have experienced temporal disorientation when they've visited the dealer's lot. Judging from early reviews and owner comments, this latest iteration of the classic pony car is destined to be every bit as successful as the one America fell in love with in 1964!

— *Brad Bowling*

1964½ MUSTANG HARDTOP

1964½ MUSTANG HARDTOP

When introduced to the public on April 17, 1964, the Mustang came in two styles — open and closed — that could be dressed up for looks or performance through an extensive option list. A media-generated buzz and a low advertised price of $2,368 helped Ford sell every Mustang it could deliver for more than a year, a success that made the career of a manager by the name of Lee Iacocca.

Although it shared a platform and several powertrains with Ford's economical Falcon line, the Mustang had a style all its own, from its recessed headlamps and forward-leaning front to the three-element taillights. The sporting theme was delivered throughout the new car's interior, as well, with sculpted bucket seats, manual floor shift and complementing colors standard. Mustang's wheelbase measured 108 inches with an overall length of 181.6 inches.

The "half-year" model designation was created by enthusiasts after the car's introduction. Ford never referred to early Mustangs as being part of a 1964½ season.

Regardless of the model year, Ford sold a staggering 120,000 Mustangs before 1965 production began.

1964½ Production Chart			
Model	**Price**	**Weight**	**Production**
07 (hardtop)	$2,368	2,449	91,532
08 (convertible)	$2,614	2,615	28,468
Year Total			120,000

1964½ MUSTANG CONVERTIBLE

1964½ MUSTANG CONVERTIBLE

Right away, the top-down crowd was won over by the new Mustang convertible, with sharp lines that were only improved in open-air mode. Ordering a drop-top Mustang cost only $246 more than a basic coupe, and an additional $54.10 made it a powered top. Ford sold 28,468 convertible Mustangs during the initial half-year season, which was nearly one-third of overall production.

Whether coupe or convertible, Ford was pleased to find customers liberally signing up for extra-cost equipment such as heaters (99 percent), whitewall tires (88 percent), radios (78 percent), windshield washers (48 percent), back-up lights (45 percent), power steering (31 percent), tinted windshields (22 percent), full tinted glass (8 percent) and air conditioning (6.4 percent).

Movie Mustangs

Its popularity with the American public made Ford's new model an instant movie star. The 1964½-'65 Mustang appeared in "Goldfinger," "A Man and a Woman" and "Beach Blanket Bingo," just to name a few.

289-CID K-CODE "HI-PO" ENGINE

K-CODE V-8

As part of its mass production system, Ford coded its Mustang powertrains with letters or numbers, which it recorded as the fifth character in the vehicle's identification number, or "VIN." For example, the base Mustang engine for 1964½ was a 170-cid inline six-cylinder wearing a one-barrel Ford Autolite carburetor that generated an advertised 101 horsepower. It was designated "U." The 260-cid two-barrel V-8 was known to Mustang folk as the "F" engine, and the letter "D" was assigned to the next plant up the ladder, a four-barrel 289-cid V-8. The first Mustangs only offered these three engines, so a U, F or D will appear as the fifth character in the VIN.

Introduced near the start of 1965 production, the 271-horsepower (or "K-code") V-8 immediately assumed its spot at the top of the Mustang must-have list for performance-minded buyers. Available only with Ford's heavy-duty four-speed manual transmission, the K-code — like the base 210-horse Mustang V-8 — was a cast-iron block bored to 289 cubic inches mated to overhead valve heads and fed by an Autolite four-barrel carburetor. The additional grunt came from a higher compression ratio (10.5:1 versus 9.0:1) and solid lifters. K-code engines are highly prized by collectors today, even though they were overshadowed later by larger displacement power plants.

Code	Engine	Intake	Power (hp)	Transmission
U	170-cid 6	1-bbl	101	M3, M4, A3
F	260-cid V-8	2-bbl	164	M3, M4, A3
D	289-cid V-8	4-bbl	210	M3, M4, A3
K	289-cid V-8	4-bbl	271	M4

1964½ Engines

SPINNER HUBCAPS

SPINNERS

The Mustang's long option list offered buyers several wheel and cover designs, but the early cars are commonly remembered for their "spinner" hubcaps. Mimicking authentic knock-off wire racing wheels, the spinners were a popular way to add a racy flair to the Mustang's sporty styling for very little money. Ford offered a total of four different spinner designs for the 1964½ through '65 Mustang, for as little as $17.82 for the least expensive type to $44.83 for simulated wire wheel hubcaps.

Base model wheels measured a tiny 13 inches in diameter, but for truly enthusiastic drivers, Ford offered a 14-inch styled steel rim whose hub was covered by a small red-centered cap. This sporty option was available only on V-8 Mustangs because those wheels were drilled to be mounted on five lugs. The six-cylinder cars came with four lugs in their wheels. Styled steel wheels could be had from the factory for an additional $119.71.

Tire technology, unfortunately, was still at the bottom of a steep evolutionary curve in 1964. The "high-performance" wheel and tire package was the stamped steel rim wearing 6.95x14-inch Red Band bias-ply rubber and was a $49.60 option.

RUNNING HORSE AND CORRAL

CORRAL

The Mustang's most enduring image is that of the galloping horse, perhaps because it was so prominently featured on the marque's first generation and in all of its advertising and promotion. All factory 1964½ to 1968 Mustangs were sold with the chrome corral dead center in the grille.

The 1969 and 1970 cars shrank the famous icon and displaced it to the extreme driver's edge of the grille.

Base 1971 to 1973 Mustangs restored the running horse emblem to its rightful status in the center, although cars ordered with the Sportlamp grille featured a much smaller version of the pony cantering across a tri-color background.

All Mustang II models from 1974 through 1978 — excluding the sportier Cobra II and King Cobra packages — were built with a traditional running horse and corral centered in the grille.

Starting with the 1979 Mustang, Ford stressed its "corporate" badging over individual marque identification, replacing the pony with the company's blue oval logo on the grille through the entire Fox-body run.

Since 1994, and including the recently released all-new 2005 models, Ford has recognized the value of its oldest brand and installed some version of the running pony on every Mustang built. The only exceptions were SVT's 1996 Cobra models.

SONNY BONO'S BARRIS-CUSTOMIZED MUSTANG

EARLY MUSTANG CUSTOMS

So enthusiastic was the public reaction to the new Mustang that California customizer George Barris immediately saw a palette for his own unique interpretation.

This Mustang, one of a pair created by Barris for pop stars Sonny & Cher in 1965, was treated to liberal amounts of chrome, pinstriping, custom paint colors and fake fur. Its hood and grille modification was a standard hot rod practice at the time. The two convertibles, both powered by V-8 engines and equipped with automatic transmissions, appeared in the 1967 camp movie classic "Good Times" starring Sonny & Cher.

Barris also created a wild Mustang for the

1965 film "Marriage on the Rocks," which starred singing legend Frank Sinatra. Known as the "Zebra" for its bizarre fake fur interior, the movie car featured a full wet bar and what were probably the world's first built-in drink holders. "Zebra" finished out its Hollywood career making occasional appearances on television's "Get Smart."

"Zebra" and "Pegasus," another Barris design, toured together during Ford's Custom Car Caravan of 1965. "Pegasus" was a simple Mustang fastback turned into a sad two-seater with an unattractive back half grafted on.

1965 MUSTANG 2+2

1965 MUSTANG 2+2

Ford added a third body to the Mustang line in the fall of 1964, a fastback known officially as the "2+2" model. Although trunk space was diminished when compared to the coupe and convertible, the fastback layout actually increased cargo capacity for the sporty Mustang driver on the go. By flattening the standard fold-down rear seat and opening an access panel into the trunk, water skis, golf clubs and any other travel gear could be stowed on a large, flat floor. "Silent-Flo" interior ventilation was augmented by manually operated sliders in the fastback's roof line.

More than any other factor, though, massaging the much-loved Mustang body into a sleek fastback form brought the marque to a new level of esteem in the American car community. The science of aerodynamics, as applied to mass-produced automobiles, was still in its early stages but consumers knew a high-tech, Space Age product when they saw it.

1965 Production Chart

Model	Price	Weight	Production
07 (hardtop)	$2,372	2,465	409,260
08 (convertible)	$2,614	2,650	73,112
09 (fastback)	$2,589	2,515	77,079
Year Total			559,451

1965 Engines

Code	Engine	Intake	Power (hp)	Transmission
T	200-cid 6	1-bbl	120	M3, M4, A3
C	289-cid V-8	2-bbl	164	M3, M4, A3
A	289-cid V-8	4-bbl	225	M3, M4, A3
K	289-cid V-8	4-bbl	271	M4

1965 MUSTANG GT CONVERTIBLE

1965 MUSTANG GT

Perhaps the most famous option package in Mustang history is the performance-oriented GT Equipment Group. Available for ordering as of March in 1965, the GT package could initially be applied only to Mustangs with four-barrel V-8 powertrains. It included a dual exhaust system with trumpet tailpipes exiting the rear valance, suspension upgrades, front disc brakes, special badging and stripes, and a unique grille treatment that added fog lamps.

Starting in 1967 the GT Equipment Group could be used to decorate even Mustangs with the base two-barrel V-8 engine.

The GT would disappear in 1969 — the victim of Ford's own Mach 1 option — but return with a vengeance in 1982 at the top of a model lineup that included the L, GL and GLX trim levels. In 1987 customer feedback encouraged Ford to break the GT out as a truly separate model from the cheaper lines with unique body panels and wheels. In the two-car 1994 lineup all coupes and convertibles with V-8 power became GTs by default. The V-6 cars were simply known as "Mustangs."

When Ford introduced its all-new 2005 design, it reassured traditionalists that its base V-8 package would once again wear GT badges.

PONY INTERIOR

PONY INTERIOR

Because it features a branded image of running horses on the seat vinyl, the Interior Decor Group is commonly referred to by enthusiasts as the "pony interior." Introduced as an option in March of 1965, the $107.08 package also included padded sun visors, unique luxury trim around interior panels, imitation wood grain and red-and-white courtesy lights built into the rears of the doors.

The imitation walnut-grain steering wheel is probably the most desirable and difficult part of the Interior Decor Package to find for restorers today. Fortunately, all components of this package have been reproduced.

The coupe, convertible and fastback had subtle differences in pony interior features. For instance, the fastback lacked any pony branding on its rear seat vinyl, but the other two body styles were stamped with the running horse design on all four seats.

Coupes featured bright trim caps at the top of the leading edge of the inside rear panel, but the other two models did not.

1965 SHELBY GT-350

1965 SHELBY GT-350

A retired racer and father of the Cobra 289, Carroll Shelby began production of a Mustang-based GT-350 in December of 1964. By arrangement with Ford, Shelby received an allotment of Wimbledon White fastbacks directly from the San Jose, California, factory with the 289-cid/271-horsepower K-code V-8. The first batch was 110 units, just more than the 100 Shelby needed to get his cars approved for production by the Sports Car Club of America (SCCA).

Running all the first year's production of GT-350s in white was done so the Ford and Shelby assembly lines could be better coordinated. White was the obvious color choice since many GT-350s would be painted for racing.

Converting the cars to GT-350s followed the racing formula: remove anything that doesn't make it faster. Many stock parts were deleted at the Ford factory or pulled at Shelby American, including hoods, exhaust systems, and decorative grille bars.

All GT-350s had fiberglass hoods, and a fiberglass shelf where the stock rear seat would be. The spare tire took the bulk of the useable room, qualifying the car as a "sports car" in the SCCA racing series. It also helped reduce weight.

Each GT-350 received a tri-bar Guardsman Blue paint stripe along the rocker panel and door bottom. The stripes broke only for a "G.T. 350" logo rendered in 3M tape. Customers could also request twin, 10-inch-wide blue racing "LeMans" stripes — a popular option that ran from front to rear over the top of the car.

According to 1965 accounts, the GT-350 was the most brutal car ever built for the public. It was beastly fast and required a heavy foot and strong arms to drive it. Unlike a race car, it could be purchased at Ford dealerships and came with a full warranty.

1965 Shelby Production Chart		
Model	**Price**	**Production**
09 (fastback GT-350)	$4,547	526
09 (fastback GT-350R)	$5,995	36
Year Total		562*

*Total includes 521 GT-350s, 34 GT-350Rs, 4 drag racing versions (with street serial numbers), 2 R-model prototypes and 1 GT-350 prototype.

1965 SHELBY GT-350 V-8 ENGINE

1965 SHELBY GT-350 POWERTRAIN AND SUSPENSION

Shelby modified Ford's stock K-code V-8 engine with a "Cobra" aluminum high-rise intake manifold, 715-cfm Holley four-barrel carburetor, "Cobra" cast aluminum finned valve covers, a "Cobra" finned cast aluminum 6.5-quart oil pan, steel tubing "Tri-Y" exhaust headers, low-restriction mufflers, and dual side-exit exhaust pipes. The advertised output for this special power plant was 306 hp.

Shelby American shored up the engine compartment with a "Monte Carlo" bar because of the engine's extra power. GT-350 suspension modifications included a thicker front sway bar, longer idler and Pitman arms, lowered upper control arms, over-ride traction bars, and Koni adjustable shock absorbers. Heavy-duty brake pads were added to the stock Mustang system. Other mechanical hard parts included a heavy-duty shortened Galaxie rear end with a Detroit Automotive no-spin gear unit and an aluminum-cased Borg-Warner T-10 four-speed transmission.

Stock wheels were stamped steel 15 x 5½-inch production pieces from Ford's big station wagons, painted silver and minus any type of hubcap. Because they looked so utilitarian, most buyers opted for the Cragar or American Racing optional rims produced to Shelby's specifications. Shelby, a Goodyear tire distributor, chose high-performance Goodyear Blue Dots to give the GT-350 the best street rubber available.

1965 Shelby Engine				
Code	Engine	Intake	Power (hp)	Transmission
K	289-cid V-8	4-bbl	306	M4

1966 MUSTANG CONVERTIBLE

1966 MUSTANG

With the most popular new car in history flying out of its showrooms, Ford changed the Mustang very little for 1966. Only minor interior and exterior trim was modified. The instrument panel was revised to end comparisons to the Falcon, a grille with a galloping pony emblem was housed in a floating corral in a background of horizontal metal strips and what some described as a "three-tooth comb" anchoring the Mustang's side cove indention.

Some feature changes reflected the new federally mandated safety standards, including front and rear seat belts; padded instrument panel; emergency flashers; electric wipers; and windshield washers as standard equipment. The list of regular Mustang features was composed of front bucket seats; pleated vinyl upholstery and interior trim; Sports-type steering wheel; five-dial instrument cluster; full carpeting; heater and defroster; left-hand door outside rearview mirror; back-up lamps; door courtesy lights; rocker panel moldings; full wheel covers; three-speed manual transmission with floor lever control; and 200-cid 120-hp six-cylinder engine. The fastback also came with special Silent-Flo ventilation, and the base V-8 was the 200-hp version of the 289-cid engine.

A series of magazine advertisements built on a Walter Mitty "daydreamer" theme helped Ford retain its sales momentum for 1966. A famous example showed a "harried accountant" who changed his lifestyle to a relaxed-looking convertible owner through the purchase of a red Mustang ragtop.

1966 Production Chart			
Model	**Price**	**Weight**	**Production**
07 (hardtop)	$2,416	2,488	499,751
08 (convertible)	$2,653	2,650	72,119
09 (fastback)	$2,607	2,519	35,698
Year Total			607,568

1966 MUSTANG SPRINT

1966 MUSTANG SPRINT

Mustangs were selling very well for Ford in 1966, but many market factors were converging to slow the car's success—starting with a higher sticker price. More standard features (some installed under new federal safety regulations) raised the prices of base Mustangs for buyers, who were asked to pay an additional $44 for the hardtop, $18 for the 2+2, and $49 for the convertible.

Americans experienced a 3.7 percent cost of living increase from 1965 to '66, and interest rates jumped to a record 5.5 percent, decreasing purchasing power a full percent and causing car sales to fall drastically in the second half of the year.

These economic forces, combined with a shortage of V-8 engines, put Ford in the position of promoting the cheaper, more efficient Mustangs over the high-performance models. The company's quick reaction to the Vietnam War-weakened economy was a run of six-cylinder "Sprint" coupes featuring special wheel covers, a distinctive accent stripe, a center console, an engine decal and a chromed air cleaner.

Advertised as Limited Edition Mustangs during the Millionth Mustang Sale (during which time buyers received a personalized dashboard nameplate), the dressed-up coupes sold in respectable numbers. The cars have some collector interest today, although there are no codes in the VIN or data plate information to identify them as Sprints.

1966 Engines				
Code	Engine	Intake	Power (hp)	Transmission
T	200-cid 6	1-bbl	120	M3, M4, A3
C	289-cid V-8	2-bbl	200	M3, M4, A3
A	289-cid V-8	4-bbl	225	M3, M4, A3
K	289-cid V-8	4-bbl	271	M4, A3

MUSTANG "GT-R" RESTO-ROD CONVERTIBLE

MUSTANG RESTO-RODS

A resto-rod is a hybrid that blends elements of old cars with components from new ones. The idea is to create a unique vehicle by combining the best traits of both. In the world of street rods, this school of thought compels otherwise normal folks to install modern Corvette motors into stock-looking 1940 Ford bodies — as classic styling meets high-tech power!

Somewhere in the recent past someone with a good set of tools and basic shade-tree mechanic skills was looking at two immobile Mustangs in his garage and thought: "I blew up the motor in my '65, and I wrecked my '95 Cobra with practically no miles on it. What to do?" The elegant solution was to throw out the junk and build one car out of what was left.

First-generation Mustangs powered by EFI-fed 5.0-liter and 4.6-liter V-8s and shifted through Borg-Warner T-5 five-speeds have gained popularity for more than a decade. Some owners go so far as to upgrade the suspension, brakes and rear axle, making the resto-rod the perfect way to enjoy old-time design and a sporty but comfortable ride at the same time.

1966 SHELBY GT-350

1966 SHELBY GT-350

Early in the 1966 Shelby production cycle, efficiency experts visited the plant to make changes to Shelby's car-building process. Some costly, time-consuming procedures performed on the 1965 GT-350 brought customer and dealer complaints. They included the expensive, clunky Detroit Locker rear axle and the super-stiff competition suspension.

Dealers wanted sporty, but comfortable, cars that could seat four people and be serviced by a regular Ford technician. They wanted a Mustang just a little faster than the factory's GT option, with more colors, an automatic transmission and a back seat. Shelby dealers also asked for a less-expensive conversion. A stripped Mustang listing for nearly $1,000 more than a loaded Galaxie turned off many potential customers.

Shelby made the Detroit Locker rear axle an option, and replaced the race-ready traction over-ride bars with easier-to-install units. Koni adjustable shocks were gradually phased out. The expensive, imported wooden steering wheels were replaced with stock Mustang GT units with GT-350 logos. The Guardsman Blue side stripes were now entirely a 3M tape product.

The 1966 GT-350 retailed for less than the 1965 at $4,428, and was a more comfortable, customer-friendly package. Amenities included Candy Apple Red, Sapphire Blue, Ivy Green, Wimbledon White and Raven Black paint; and a C-4 high-performance automatic transmission option (a 595-cfm carburetor was specified with the automatic). An AM radio became a factory-installed option halfway through the year.

Shelby offered a factory-installed Paxton supercharger for $670 toward the end of the model year. The company claimed the option produced up to 46 percent more horsepower from the 289-cid V-8. Shelby blowers had a warranty only for 90 days or 4,000 miles. Only 11 GT-350s were ordered with this high-performance option.

1966 Shelby Production Chart		
Model	**Price**	**Production**
09 (fastback GT-350)	$4,428	2,374
08 (convertible GT-350)	N/A	4
Year Total		2,378*
*Total includes 1,369 GT-350s, 1,001 Hertz models, 4 convertibles and 4 drag racing versions.		

1966 SHELBY GT-350H

1966 SHELBY GT-350H

Sales to Hertz (for its Sports Car Club) accounted for nearly 40 percent of Shelby American's 1966 production. A special run of 1001 GT-350H fastbacks was put into service as rental cars — mostly in black-with-gold paint schemes, but later in all 1966 Shelby colors. Early H-models included all of the heavy-duty suspension modifications. Hertz later asked that all of its GT-350s come with automatic transmissions and a brake booster for the stiff competition-style brakes.

Receiving the Hertz order was probably the pivotal point in Shelby production. Guaranteeing nearly 1,000 cars (the original pitch to Hertz executives was for 100 units) put Shelby American in a better position to bargain with its suppliers.

The sale also meant that the average traveler could be exposed to the GT-350, a point that no doubt increased non-Hertz sales for 1966 and later. Featuring the GT-350 in all of Hertz' national advertising didn't hurt, either.

1966 Shelby Engine				
Code	Engine	Intake	Power (hp)	Transmission
K	289-cid V-8	4-bbl	306	M4, A3

1967 PLAYBOY PINK MUSTANG HARDTOP

1967 MUSTANG

Ford had dominated the pony car market by using the element of surprise to its advantage in 1964, but several automakers were finally getting competitive by 1967 with Chevrolet's Camaro, Pontiac's Firebird (introduced six months behind its sister Camaro), and Mercury's Mustang-based Cougar, among others. Ford responded with its first redesign of the Mustang featuring a jazzy new body, a wider track for better road grip, a broader range of engines, and a longer options list.

Mustang designers retained the original styling theme, but made everything larger for 1967, starting with the grille's more pronounced opening. Larger simulated scoops dominated the car's side, and three vertical taillight lenses were on each side of a concave indentation panel, with a centrally located gas cap. The overall appearance was more muscular. The wheelbase was unchanged, but overall length grew by nearly two inches. Front and rear tread widths went up by 2.1 inches and overall width increased 2.7 inches to 70.9 inches. The new 2+2 fastback was especially sleek, with its roofline displaying a clean, unbroken sweep rearward to a distinctive,

concave rear panel. Functional air louvers in the rear quarters became thinner.

The Mustang included all Ford safety features as standard equipment, plus front bucket seats, full carpeting, a floor-mounted shifter, vinyl interior trim, heater, wheel covers and cigarette lighter. The fastback came with wheel covers, special emblems and rocker panel moldings.

Even the popular Mustang could not fight the American economic slowdown in 1967. Instead of selling nine million units industry-wide, Ford's final sales figures fell by a million cars from the previous year. Total Mustang production for 1967 was 472,121 units, with the company managing to increase V-8 production by 20 percent. Special promotions boosted air conditioning installations to 16 percent, a 6.5 percent increase.

1967 Production Chart

Model	Price	Weight	Production
01 (hardtop)	$2,461	2,578	356,271
02 (fastback)	$2,592	2,605	71,042
03 (convertible)	$2,698	2,738	44,808
Year Total			472,121

1967 MUSTANG GTA

1967 MUSTANG GTA

In 1967, knowing there was competition for its performance-oriented Mustang on the way, Ford squeezed big-block power in the pony's engine compartment — a 390-cid, 320-hp plant that provided neck-snapping street thrills and some dragstrip bragging rights for only $264. The 390 was a small-bore/long-stroke member of the "FE" family Ford introduced in 1958.

For one year only, adding an automatic transmission (now capable of manual shifts) to the Mustang's GT Equipment Group created a "GTA" model. Available only with one of the four V-8s, the GT package included four-inch driving lamps, power front disc brakes, low-restriction dual exhausts with quad outlets, GT rocker panel stripes, GT or GTA emblem, F70x14 whitewall tires, GT gas cap and special handling equipment such as higher rate springs and shocks, and a larger front stabilizer bar.

Budget-minded buyers were not overlooked

in '67. Ford produced the Sports Sprint that spring which included sporty hood vents with recessed turn indicators; whitewalls; full wheel covers; bright rocker panel moldings; a chrome air cleaner; and a vinyl-covered shift lever if SelectShift Cruise-O-Matic transmission was ordered. In addition, Sports Sprint buyers were tempted with a special price on factory-installed SelectAire air conditioning.

Available in hardtop and convertible styles, the Sports Sprint was offered in a "Ford's better ideas for sale" promotion that pitched "1968 ideas at 1967 prices."

1967 Engines				
Code	Engine	Intake	Power (hp)	Transmission
T	200-cid 6	1-bbl	120	M3, A3
C	289-cid V-8	2-bbl	200	M3, M4, A3
A	289-cid V-8	4-bbl	225	M3, M4, A3
K	289-cid V-8	4-bbl	271	M4, A3
S	390-cid V-8	4-bbl	320	M4, A3

1967 MUSTANG "T-5" CONVERTIBLE

T-5

Mustangs were not just an American success story, because pony fever was international in scope!

Holland's Ford factory, for example, produced Mustang coupes for domestic sales during model years 1965 and '66, while other European countries imported the cars from the United States.

In Germany, Ford found that Krupp, the steel company that had once provided industrial muscle and armaments to Hitler's war machine, had trademarked the name Mustang for a line of heavy-duty trucks it produced from 1951 to 1964. Kreidler, a manufacturer of motorcycles and scooters from 1951 to 1983, also had registered the name for one of its off-road two-wheelers, which further complicated Ford's effort to sell Mustangs to Germany. Rather than pay Krupp and Kreidler $10,000 for their cooperation, Ford reverted to its early project code name and replaced all "Mustang" badging on the cars with "T-5" emblems.

T-5s were not substantially different from Mustangs sold in the U.S. market, but modifications fluctuated based on the eventual customer. For example, cars sold to American military personnel were usually ordered with speedometers and odometers reading in standard miles while German citizens took delivery of Mustangs calibrated for kilometers. Early T-5s (this practice ran from 1964 through the start of 1979 model production) received heavy-duty suspensions to handle Europe's rougher road surfaces. Cars were fitted with export braces to stiffen the front part of the chassis and higher capacity radiators were installed.

Headlights, turn signals, emergency flashers and parking lamps had to meet Germany's stricter safety standards, and T-5 literature listed front disc brakes as standard equipment.

Because they are oddities in the Mustang world, collectors covet the small number of T-5s that returned to the U.S. with service personnel.

1967 SHELBY GT-500

1967 SHELBY GT-350 AND GT-500

The 1967 GT-350 and the new GT-500 distanced themselves from the stock Mustang appearance (fixing one complaint Shelby dealers had about the first-generation cars). The Shelbys became mechanically more similar to the Mustangs. Shelby dealers were happy to sell a visually exciting product with creature comforts of a basic Mustang, but without the specialized maintenance and training.

Redesigned in 1967, Shelby American's new appearance package cleverly made the fastbacks look longer and lower than stock Mustangs using more fiberglass. The new fiberglass hood wore twin scoops and racing-style lock-down pins. It made the grille look like a dark, menacing mouth. The grille opening housed the Shelby's two round high-beam headlights placed side-by-side in the middle, a style not appreciated by some states' transportation departments. The Mustang front bumper, minus the vertical bumperettes, seemed made for the Shelby. In front of each rear wheel well were fiberglass, forward-facing scoops that channeled air into the rear brakes.

Stock Mustang rear vents were covered with a rear-facing scoop that helped draw air out of the passenger compartment. (Early 1967 cars had a red running light installed in this scoop, dropped later due to legal concerns.) A three-piece spoiler was applied to the rear of all 1967 Shelby-Mustangs, accented by the extra-wide taillights mounted in a flat panel.

Ford's Deluxe Interior was chosen for the luxurious 1967 Shelbys, and was available in Black, White or Parchment. A sporty two- or four-point rollbar was installed in every car with a jet fighter-style inertia reel shoulder harness. All Shelbys received a unique wood-rimmed steering wheel. Fold-down rear seats were made standard equipment. Stewart-Warner oil pressure and amp gauges were housed under the dashboard. The Mustang's optional 8,000-rpm tach sat next to a 140-mph speedometer.

1967 Shelby Production Chart		
Model	**Price**	**Production**
02 (fastback GT-350)	$3,995	1,175
02 (fastback GT-500)	$4,195	2,048
Year Total		3,225*

*Total includes 2,048 GT-500s, 1,175 GT-350s and 2 GT-500 prototypes (a notchback and a convertible).

1967 SHELBY GT-350 V-8

1967 SHELBY GT-350 AND GT-500 POWER-TRAIN AND SUSPENSION

Although it received a new Shelby-specific code in the VIN, the 289-cid Ford K-code engine received very few changes in 1967. Tubular exhaust headers were exchanged at the beginning of the year for Ford's high-performance cast-iron manifold, yet the factory continued to claim an output of 306 horsepower. Paxton's powerful supercharger remained on the option list, as did SelectAire air conditioning and the high-performance C-4 automatic transmission. For the second straight year, GT-350 prices decreased, perhaps explaining how Shelby dealers were able to part with 1,175 units for $3,995 apiece.

With new looks came the GT-500, an addition to the Shelby line whose main attribute was big-block V-8 power. When Ford started installing its 390-cid V-8 in a Mustang at the beginning of 1967, Shelby went one better by shoehorning the 428-cid V-8 into his top-line offering. The massive powerplant produced at least 50 more horsepower than the 390. This "Police Interceptor" engine featured hydraulic lifters and an aluminum, medium-rise intake manifold wearing a pair of 600-cfm four-barrel Holley carburetors. Ford's four-speed "toploader" transmission was standard with the 1967s, with the stout "police spec" C-6 handling automatic shifting duties. The GT-500, available only in fastback form like the GT-350, retailed for $4,195 and sold 2,050 units.

Shelbys came standard that year with power steering and power-assisted brakes. Suspension enhancements were largely stock Mustang, including the special handling package, front disc brakes, thicker front stabilizer bar, export brace and adjustable Gabriel shock absorbers. Stock wheels were 15-inch stamped steel units with 1967 Thunderbird hubcaps — their identity changed with Shelby center caps. Various sporty rims from Kelsey-Hayes were optional.

1967 Shelby Engines				
Code	Engine	Intake	Power (hp)	Transmission
2	289-cid V-8	4-bbl	306	M4, A3
4	428-cid V-8	4-bbl	355	M4, A3

SHELBY 10-SPOKE WHEEL

SHELBY
10-SPOKE WHEEL

Shelby Mustangs were sold as bare-bones street racers in 1965 and early 1966, so not many buyers were put off by the silver 15 x 5.5-inch stamped steel station wagon wheels that came standard on each GT-350. Customers with deeper pockets preferred the optional chromed 15-inch five-spoke Cragar mag wheel.

Increasing the creature comfort level during '66, Shelby made a 14-inch Magnum 500 with gray finish standard, and a 14-inch aluminum 10-spoke design optional. GT-350s destined for the Hertz Rent-A-Racer program were fitted with chrome-finished Magnums.

Shelby continued its preference for standard 15-inch steel wheels in 1967 and 1968, but covered with '67 Thunderbird hubcaps wearing Shelby-branded centers. Early in 1967 the optional wheel was a 15-inch five-spoke Kelsey-Hayes "MagStar" design that featured aluminum centers attached to chromed steel rims. Shelby introduced a wheel of its own design (and some would say its most elegant) as an option late in 1967— the 15 x 7-inch aluminum 10-spoke.

Shelby's standard wheel for the 1969-'70 season was a new 15 x 7-inch five-spoke with an aluminum center attached to a chromed steel rim. Inadequate machining on some early 1969 Shelby wheels forced a recall for inspection and testing.

Like most parts for classic Mustangs, Shelby wheels have been reproduced and are readily available for the restorer or modifier.

1968 MUSTANG 2+2

1968 MUSTANG

1968 was another milestone year for federally mandated equipment on Mustangs, the most obvious addition to the exterior being side marker reflectors. The Mustang interior underwent its most dramatic upgrade, with a safer, energy-absorbing steering wheel and a new seatbelt system incorporating a shoulder harness on coupes and fastbacks. The standard bucket seats (and extra-cost bench units) received locking mechanisms to keep the backs from flopping forward when the car braked.

Ford modified the 1968 front end with the pony and corral now "floating" in the grille. Also, script-style (instead of block letter) Mustang body side nameplates; and cleaner-looking bright metal trim on the cove replaced the previous "cheese grater" fake scoops. Rear view mirrors were attached directly to the windshield with adhesive, and an optional collapsible spare tire increased usable storage space in the trunk.

The $147 GT Equipment Group remained popular with its characteristic stripe along the bottom of the door line or a reflecting "C" design that widened along the ridge of the front

fender and ran across the door, to the upper rear body quarter. From there, it turned down, around the sculptured depression ahead of the rear wheel, and tapered forward, along the lower body to about the mid-point of the door. The GT package also included auxiliary lights in the grille, a GT gas cap, and GT wheel covers. On the 1968 Mustang, the extra lights no longer had a bar separating them from the corral. Extra cost front disc brakes were standard when big-block V-8s were ordered. 17,458 GTs were made in 1968.

While the Mustang was still the best-selling pony car in America, it slipped from second place in 1965 to seventh place in 1968. A 60-day strike against Ford from late September to late November of 1967 had a negative effect on Mustang sales and production.

1968 Production Chart			
Model	**Price**	**Weight**	**Production**
01 (hardtop)	$2,602	2,635	249,447
02 (fastback)	$2,712	2,659	42,325
03 (convertible)	$2,814	2,745	25,376
Year Total			317,148

1968 289-CID V-8 ENGINE

1968 MUSTANG 428 COBRA JET

It was a very unusual April Fools' Day present in 1968 when Ford Motor Co. introduced the 428-cid Cobra Jet V-8 to its Mustang line. The 335-horsepower package that changed the Mustang from sporty pony car to dragstrip terror was available with a three-speed automatic or four-speed manual transmission. All 428 CJs for 1968 were fastbacks with the GT Equipment Group, heavy-duty handling equipment and Mustang's first functional hood scoop. They could quickly be identified by a wide, non-reflective black stripe that ran the length of the hood.

Other new engines included a 302-cid V-8 rated at 230 hp when equipped with a four-barrel carburetor and 220 hp when wearing a two-barrel. A 390-cid V-8 with 325 hp was a new "FE" family engine first offered in the Mustang in 1967. The 200-cid six and base 289-cid V-8 were standard, but their ratings dropped to 115 and 195 hp, respectively.

1968 Engines				
Code	Engine	Intake	Power (hp)	Transmission
T	200-cid 6	1-bbl	115	M3, A3
C	289-cid V-8	2-bbl	195	M3, M4, A3
F	302-cid V-8	2-bbl	220	M3, M4, A3
J	302-cid V-8	4-bbl	230	M3, M4, A3
X	390-cid V-8	2-bbl	280	M3, M4, A3
S	390-cid V-8	4-bbl	325	M3, M4, A3
R	428-cid V-8	4-bbl	335	M4, A3

1968 CALIFORNIA SPECIAL GT/CS

1968 MUSTANG CALIFORNIA SPECIAL

West Coast Ford dealers promoted a very unusual Mustang package in 1968. It was the Shelby-influenced GT/CS California Special. Available only in coupe form, the GT/CS included a Shelby-style deck lid with a spoiler, sequential taillights, and a blacked-out grille (minus Mustang identification). Wheel covers were the same ones used on 1968 GTs, but without GT identification. Five thousand Mustangs were planned with this package, which was inspired by "Little Red," a 1967 coupe prototype produced by Carroll Shelby.

When predicted sales figures were not met, production was scaled back and only 4,325 units were built.

A much smaller number of similar High Country Specials was built for Denver dealers following the completion of the California models. All GT/CS and High Country cars were built at the San Jose Ford plant.

1968 SHELBY GT-500

1968 SHELBY GT-350 & GT-500

In 1968, Shelby production was relocated to Michigan because the best source for high-volume fiberglass parts was nearby in Canada. The A.O. Smith Co., in Ionia, Mich., experienced with large-volume conversions and working with fiberglass, manufactured all 1968 Shelbys from Mustang fastbacks and convertibles assembled at Ford's Metuchen, New Jersey, plant.

Shelby's GT-350s and GT-500s received cosmetic changes. The hood now featured twin scoops running almost to the leading edge of the car. The stock Mustang hood lock mechanism was retained, although external turn-knob fasteners were provided. An even larger "mouth" was created with an all-new fiberglass front valance panel. That mouth housed twin rectangular Marchal driving lights, later replaced with Lucas units. It was the first time an American production car came with factory-installed auxiliary driving lights. Wide, sequential taillights from the 1965 Thunderbird just about stretched the width of the car's rear panel.

Ford's 302-cid V-8 (based on the 260/289 block) was new under the hood, rated at 250 hp, down 56 from the previous model. Early production cars breathed through a 600-cfm Autolite carburetor sitting on a cast-iron intake manifold. An aluminum Cobra intake went into the mix once certification was complete. The GT-500 got a 428-cid/360-hp version of Ford's Police Interceptor package. A few 390-cid V-8s were installed when the 428 ran short. The 428 had a single 735-cfm Holley four-barrel carburetor, but it (and the GT-350) had air cleaners sporting two screw-down wing nuts suggesting two carburetors were hiding there.

One-third of all 1968 Shelby conversions were performed on convertibles.

1968 Shelby Production Chart		
Model	**Price**	**Production**
02 (fastback GT-350)	$4,116	1,227
03 (convertible GT-350)	$4,238	404
02 (fastback GT-500)	$4,317	1,046
03 (convertible GT-500)	$4,438	402
02 (fastback GT-500KR)	$4,472	1,053
03 (convertible GT-500KR)	$4,594	518
Year Total		4,451*
*Total includes 1 GT-500 coupe prototype.		

1968 SHELBY GT-500KR FASTBACK

1968 GT-500KR

In 1968, racetracks were no longer the intended habitat of Shelby's wildlife, but horsepower proliferation was still very evident when Shelby introduced the GT-500KR midyear as a replacement for the GT-500. The KR ("King of the Road" some sources claim) managed to fit Ford's new (unofficially rated) 400 hp 428 Cobra Jet between the fenders. To support such a powerful engine, extra bracing on the lower edge of the shock towers and staggered rear shocks were installed when the KR was equipped with a four-speed transmission. Wider rear brake shoes and drums, heavy-duty wheel cylinders and brake line fittings were installed for the sake of safety, as was a freer-flowing exhaust system. As with the standard GT-500, the KR was available in either fastback or convertible body style.

At the end of Shelby's best-ever year, the company produced 4,451 cars. The breakdown included 1,027 GT-350 fastbacks, 404 GT-350 convertibles, 1,046 GT-500 fastbacks, 402 GT-500 convertibles, 1,053 GT-500KR fastbacks, 518 GT-500KR convertibles and 1 notchback prototype GT-500.

Code	Engine	Intake	Power (hp)	Transmission
		1968 Shelby Engines		
J	302-cid V-8	4-bbl	250	M4, A3
S	428-cid V-8	4-bbl	360	M4, A3
R	428-cid V-8	4-bbl	335	M4, A3

1969 MUSTANG GT CONVERTIBLE

1969 MUSTANG

Ford featured an array of engines, trim levels and models for its 1969 Mustang line. It was the peak of a frenzied performance war waged against Chevrolet, Oldsmobile, Dodge — and with itself! Some participants, such as Carroll Shelby, felt that Ford was supporting too many choices in the enthusiast marketplace and the overlap of models was detrimental to the automaker's market goals.

The Mustang stable included the Mach 1, GT, Boss 302, Boss 429, Shelby GT-350 and Shelby GT-500 — all high-performance models built from the same basic platform. The cars were available with nine V-8 power plants that included an "economy" 302-cid unit, the awesome 302-cid Boss motor, a 351-cid Windsor, a 351-cid Cleveland, a final-year 390-cid, a 428-cid Cobra Jet, a 428-cid Super Cobra Jet, a 429-cid in "wedge head" form, and the ground-pounding 429-cid Boss plant.

This proliferation of models may have reflected the short but significant influence former General Motors star Semon "Bunkie" Knudsen exercised on the Ford family of cars in 1969. Knudsen, who became president of Ford Motor Company in February of 1968 after resigning as a GM executive vice president, had gained notoriety for his 11th-hour transformation of the 1957 Pontiac from an "old maid's" car into a youth-oriented machine.

With such a variety of big-block V-8s, the 1969 Mustang was also larger than ever to accommodate such power plants. The new Mustang wheelbase remained the same as previous ponies at 108 inches, but overall length grew by 3.8 inches. The Mustang's profile was sleeker than ever, with a steeply raked windshield. Quad round headlamps were used for the first (and only) time on a production Mustang in 1969. The outer lenses were recessed into the fender openings, while the inboard units were set into the grille ends.

The earlier Mustang's pinched-waist design disappeared in '69, replaced by a feature line that ran from the tip of the front fender to just behind the rear door seam. On convertibles and coupes, a rear-facing, non-functional air vent sat just in front of the rear wheel opening. Fastbacks featured a backwards C-shaped scoop.

*1969 MUSTANG
428-CID V-8 ENGINE*

1969 MUSTANG GT POWERTRAINS

The GT Equipment Group suffered a slow death in 1969, facing stiff competition from the new Mach 1 performance package. Only 4,973 coupes, convertibles and fastbacks were ordered as GTs. The few that were built cost buyers $147 for the option, which was not available in combination with the Grandé coupes, six-cylinder engines or base 302 V-8.

The standard GT engine was a 351-cid Windsor V-8 with 250 horsepower. Mustangs ordered with the GT package also got special handling equipment, lower body racing stripes, dual exhausts, pin-type hood lock latches, simulated hood scoop with integral turn signal indicators (shaker scoop with the 428CJ Ram Air V-8), three-speed manual transmission, four-wheel drum brakes, glass-belted white sidewall tires, and styled steel wheels.

The awesome Cobra Jet 428-cid V-8, introduced midway through the 1968 season, appeared again as a Mustang option. It was available with either the GT or Mach 1 package in Cobra Jet (CJ-428) or Super Cobra Jet (SCJ-428) form. The base Cobra Jet generated 335 hp at 5200 rpm and 440 lbs.-ft. of torque at 3400 rpm, while the SCJ was the same engine with Ram Air induction, a hardened steel cast crankshaft, special "LeMans" connecting rods and improved balancing for drag racing. It had the same advertised horsepower but was more powerful. *Hot Rod* magazine called a CJ-equipped Mustang "the fastest running pure stock in the history of man."

A total of 81.5 percent of 1969 Mustangs came equipped with V-8s. The other 18.5 percent contained two six-cylinder options, including a new 250-cid six with 155 hp. Automatic transmission installations ran just over 71 percent, but four-speed manual gearboxes (wide- or close-ratio) were found in nearly 11 percent.

1969 Production Chart			
Model	**Price**	**Weight**	**Production**
01 (hardtop)	$2,618	2,690	127,954
01 (hardtop Grandé)	$2,849	2,981	22,182
02 (fastback)	$2,618	2,713	61,980
02 (fastback Mach 1)	$3,122	3,175	72,458
03 (convertible)	$2,832	2,800	14,746
Year Total			299,824

1969 MUSTANG SPORTSROOF

1969 MUSTANG SPORTSROOF

Ford designers took the Mustang fastback design to a new level in 1969. Not only did the roofline of the new "SportsRoof" share nothing with the coupe, but the car's side treatment was also unique. Whereas the coupe and convertible had large fake vertical scoops below the beltline (reminiscent of the 1965-1968 cove treatment), the fastback featured a cleaner look with a much smaller non-functional air intake just below the pop-out rear quarter window. The 1969 SportsRoof was .9 inches lower than earlier fastbacks, but by allowing the panel to run the entire length of the body from the windshield rearward, stylists gave the car the illusion of a more severely lowered, or "chopped," top.

Semon Knudsen, the new president of Ford in 1968, was personally enamored with fastback body styling, and he saw the SportsRoof as the foundation for a series of hot-performing "buzz bombs." Eager to put his ideas to work immediately, he hired GM designer Larry Shinoda to create the ultimate fastback performance package — the race-inspired Boss 302.

The SportsRoof was such a huge hit for Ford that it accounted for 134,438 units out of that year's sales total of 299,824 Mustangs—a 44.8 percent slice of the pie. More than half of those were equipped with the Mach 1 package.

1969 MUSTANG QUAD HEADLIGHTS

QUAD HEADLIGHTS

In the late 1960s automotive designers were limited to three choices when it came to installing headlights on a car: put on two round ones, four round ones or hide them. Squares and rectangles had not been approved for use in North America by the likes of Sylvania and GE. And the auto industry was just learning about new ideas like halogen bulbs and wraparound housings.

The 1965 through 1968 Mustangs looked great with their two round eyes. Each provided a dull — but standard for the time — yellowish low beam and a higher-output, elevated high beam. For the 1969 Mustang, stylists created several front end design prototypes on paper and in clay where the headlamps would be hidden behind a foldaway body panel similar to the treatment on GM's 1965 Buick Riviera and what the Mercury division had executed with the 1967 Cougar. The major drawback to the hideaway headlights occurred in climates where ice could seal the doors shut at the most inopportune times.

Design exercises for four-headlight systems were eventually chosen because they gave the large 1969 Mustang a ready-to-race look Ford had achieved on its earlier models through the addition of the GT fog lamp package. Most Americans had seen enough European rallies on television and in magazines to know that only serious competitors needed more than two lights on the fronts of their cars. Hence, the appeal of Shelby's 1967 GT-350 and GT-500 with their standard grille-mounted auxiliary illumination.

So novel was Ford's four-light system that each 1969 Mustang came with a set of adapters for mechanics to use when aligning the two inboard units.

The 1970 Mustang returned to the earlier style of having two round headlights—a format retained through the end of Mustang II production in 1978.

1969 MUSTANG MACH 1

1969 MACH 1

After its introduction late in 1968, it was clear the Mach 1 would become the Mustang's most popular performance upgrade ever, with its matte black hood, simulated hood scoop, and exposed NASCAR-style hood lock pins (which could be deleted) and extra-cost black rear spoiler. A reflective side stripe and rear stripes carried the model designation just behind the front wheel arches and above the chrome pop-up gas cap. Chrome styled steel wheels and chrome exhausts tips (when optional four-barrel carburetors were ordered) were other bright touches. Also featured were dual color-keyed racing mirrors, and a handling suspension.

Interior appointments were many for the Mach 1, which featured high-back bucket seats; black carpets; a Rim-Blow steering wheel; center console; clock; sound-deadening insulation; and teakwood-grained trim on the doors, dash and console.

The base engine was a 351-cid two-barrel Windsor V-8 — essentially a stroked 302-cid Ford V-8 with raised deck height which created a great street performance powerplant. Optional engines included the 351-cid 290-hp four-barrel V-8 and a 390-cid 320-hp V-8.

"Mustang Mach 1 — holder of 295 land speed records," proclaimed the 1969 Performance Buyer's Digest. "This is the one that Mickey Thompson started with. From its wide-oval, belted tires to its wind tunnel-designed SportsRoof, the word is 'go.'" The copy pointed out the production car had "the same wind-splitting sheet metal as the specially modified Mach 1 that screamed around Bonneville clocking over 155, hour after hour, to break some 295 USAC speed and endurance records."

Ad lines:

Ford for '69 – It's the Going Thing!

Mustang Mach 1 – A Horse of a Different Color

Ford's Fine Line of Cars Never Stops Rolling

Nearest Thing to a Trans-Am Mustang that You Can Bolt a License Plate Onto – Boss 302

1969 MUSTANG GRANDÉ

1969 GRANDÉ

Realizing there was competition hungry for market share, Ford played dress-up with all of its 1969 body styles to remind buyers the Mustang was—as introductory ads had touted — "designed to be designed by you."

Fastbacks could be had in a variety of flavors, the most popular being the new Mach 1. Convertibles were likewise available from plain to packed. For 1969 even the bread-and-butter hardtop, which historically outsold fastbacks and convertibles, was given its own unique package in the form of the Grandé, which offered a vinyl roof, plush interior, deluxe two-spoke steering wheel, color-keyed racing mirrors, full wheel covers, electric clock, bright exterior body moldings, dual outside paint stripes, and luxury foam bucket seats for only $231 above the normal hardtop with comparable equipment.

In its first year, Grandé production accounted for only 7 percent of all Mustang sales, but 17 percent of all hardtop units. That was enough for Ford to keep offering the package through the end of 1973.

1969 Engines				
Code	Engine	Intake	Power (hp)	Transmission
T	200-cid 6	1-bbl	115	M3, A3
L	250-cid 6	1-bbl	155	M3, A3
F	302-cid V-8	2-bbl	220	M3, M4, A3
G (Boss)	302-cid V-8	4-bbl	290	M4
H	351-cid V-8	2-bbl	250	M3, M4, A3
M	351-cid V-8	4-bbl	290	M3, M4, A3
S	390-cid V-8	4-bbl	320	M4, A3
Q (CJ)	428-cid V-8	4-bbl	335	M4, A3
R (SCJ)	428-cid V-8	4-bbl	360	M4, A3
Z (Boss)	429-cid V-8	4-bbl	370	M4

1969 MUSTANG BOSS 302

1969 BOSS 302

Articles in 1969-era car magazines said Ford's new-for-1969 Boss 302 out-classed "most of the world's big-engined muscle cars." Other reports hinted a slightly modified Boss 302 engine would keep increasing power all the way to a stratospheric 8,000 rpm, which suggested that some owners were bypassing the rpm limiter. Ford's peak horsepower rating of 290 at 5800 rpm was conservative. It was Ford's answer to the Camaro Z28 on the Sports Car Club of America's Trans-American racing circuit and a worthy competitor in the showroom.

The Boss 302 suspension received competition-quality, high-rate (350 inch-pounds) springs; heavy-duty direct-acting Gabriel shock absorbers; and a steel stabilizer bar with specifically calibrated rubber mounts. The Hotchkiss-type rear suspension had 150 inch-pound leaf springs and staggered shock absorbers to control wheel hop and bounce. Ford also added a rear stabilizer bar for improved cornering.

Axle ratios included the standard 3.50:1 non-locking unit, but buyers could order a Traction-Lok 3.50:1 and 3.91:1. There was also a No-Spin axle available with a 4.30:1 ratio built by Detroit Automotive. To prevent buildup of stress points in the axle shafts, Ford installed fully machined units with larger axle shaft splines, an extra-strength cast nodular iron center section, and larger wheel seals.

The Boss 302 brake system included discs in the front and power assist. Power steering was available as an option. Details included black in the taillamp bezels; chrome backlight moldings; and the hood, rear deck lid and lower back panel.

The Boss interior was still basic Mustang with circular gauges, dash lights to monitor oil pressure and electrical systems, and a tachometer. Desirable Boss options were an adjustable rear deck lid spoiler and rear window SportSlats. To qualify as a production model by Trans-Am racing rules, Ford was required to produce a minimum of 1,000 Boss 302 Mustangs. The car's popularity racked up 1,628 sales in 1969.

1969 Boss 302 Production Chart			
Model	**Price**	**Weight**	**Production**
02 (fastback Boss 302)	$3,354	3,250	1,628

1969 MUSTANG BOSS 302 G-CODE V-8

1969 BOSS 302 POWERTRAIN

The V-8 that motivated the 1969 Boss 302 was the ultimate evolution of the 260- and 289-cid Mustang V-8s. Introduced in 1965, it had special cylinder heads that gave it a performance advantage over the previous small-block Mustangs. This "Cleveland" valve train (so called because of the similarity to those used on the 351-cid engine made in Ford's Cleveland, Ohio, foundry) used canted intake and exhaust valves that permitted the fitting of bigger ports and valves and a straighter flowing fuel/air mixture that gave better volumetric efficiency.

Boss 302 intake valves measured a massive 2.23 inches in 1969, and exhaust valves were 1.71 inches, incredibly large for a production small-block engine. Semi-hemispherical combustion chambers were also different from those of the earlier small-blocks, with a wedge design that resembled the shape of the chambers in the Ford 427-cid V-8 racing engine. The camshaft had 290 degrees of duration for both valves and a .290-inch lift. The crankshaft, balanced both statically and dynamically (with the rods and pistons in place), was made of forged steel to stand up to high rpms. Forged steel connecting rods were used. Other features included a high-rise, aluminum intake manifold with a single 780-cfm four-barrel Holley carburetor; pop-up type pistons; a dual-point distributor; a high-pressure oil pump; lightweight, stamped rocker arms; screw-in rocker arm studs and pushrod guide plates (with specially hardened pushrods); an oil pan windage baffle and screw-in freeze plugs.

Ford wisely chose to install only manual transmissions in the Boss 302, with a floor-mounted Hurst shifter handling shifting chores.

1969 Boss 302 Engine			
Code	**Engine**	**Power (hp)**	**Transmission**
G	302-cid V-8	290	M4

1969 BOSS 429

1969 BOSS 429

The more powerful stablemate to the Boss 302, the Boss 429 was created because Ford had still another engine it wanted to place into competition, this time on the NASCAR circuit. Ford decided to install the new-for-1969 429-cid "semi-hemi" big-block in the popular Mustang platform. That followed predictions that it would be easier to sell 500 such models than a Torino-based super car. Kar Kraft, an aftermarket firm in Brighton, Michigan, was contracted to build Boss 429s. Because the Mustang's engine compartment was not designed to house such a wide engine, the job required a big shoehorn and a lot of suspension changes and chassis modifications.

Body alterations to the Boss 429 included engine bay bracing, inner wheel well sheet metal work, and flared wheel housings to accommodate a widened track and the use of seven-inch Magnum 500 rims. The hood was topped by a huge, functional scoop and a unique spoiler underlined the front bumper. Power steering and brakes, a Traction-Lok axle with 3.91 gears, and the Boss 302's rear spoiler were also included. Boss 429s came equipped with the fancy Decor Group interior option plus high-back bucket seats, deluxe seat belts, wood-trimmed dash and console treatment and Visibility Group option. Automatic transmission and air conditioning were not available, but the $3,826 price tag included all of the above.

Horsepower for the Boss 429 was advertised as 375, although real ratings were rumored to be much higher. A total of 1,358 Boss 429s were constructed during the 1969 calendar year. This included 859 of the 1969 models made in early 1969 and 499 1970 models built late in the summer.

1969 Boss 429 Production Chart			
Model	**Price**	**Weight**	**Production**
02 (fastback Boss 429)	$3,826	3,530	859

1970 SHELBY GT-350 CONVERTIBLE

1969 & 1970 SHELBY GT-350 AND GT-500

The third-generation Shelby Mustang went full circle in relation to the stock Ford product. In 1965, the GT-350 looked exactly like a Mustang, but underneath beat the hot rod heart of a race car. In 1969, the GT-350 didn't even resemble the stock pony car in silhouette, but its mechanical DNA was pure Mustang. The 1969 Shelby was further camouflaged through the use of fiberglass; composite fenders, hood, and rear cap. All that allowed Shelby designers to stretch the GT-350 another three inches past the already-elongated 1969 Mustangs.

The GT-350/500 hood was festooned with five recessed NASA-type hood scoops, with the leading edge trimmed with a chrome strip that curved at the outer edges to meet the unique-to-Shelby front bumper. A chrome strip formed a wide rectangle inside the car's "mouth" as it ran around the outside of the flat black grille. Lucas driving lights were again chosen.

The beltlines of the fastback and convertible bodies were decorated with traditional Shelby stripes. Working rear brake cooling scoops stood out just ahead of the rear wheel well.

1965 Thunderbird sequential taillights, further removed the cars from their Mustang roots. Directly between the two taillight lenses sat a spring-mounted frame that displayed the license plate and concealed the fuel filler cap.

Paint colors for 1969 offered the greatest choice in Shelby history, with all of Ford's "Grabber" hues available. Bright Blue, Green, Yellow, Orange and Competition Orange were added early in the year to Black Jade, Acapulco Blue, Gulfstream Aqua, Pastel Gray, Candy Apple Red and Royal Maroon.

1969-'70 Shelby Production Chart		
Model	**Price**	**Production**
02 (fastback GT-350)	$4,434	935
02 (fastback GT-350H)	N/A	152
03 (convertible GT-350)	$4,753	194
02 (fastback GT-500)	$4,709	1,534
03 (convertible GT-500)	$5,027	335
Year Total		3,153*

*Total includes 3 barrier test and pilot cars. Records indicate that 789 cars were sold as 1970 models, although there is currently no accurate body style breakdown.

1970 SHELBY GT-500 428-CID V-8

1969-70 SHELBY GT-350 & GT-500 POWERTRAIN & SUSPENSION

Every GT-350 built in 1969 received Ford's new 351-cid 290-hp Windsor V-8 that breathed through a 470-cfm Autolite four-barrel carburetor and came standard attached to Ford's four-speed manual transmission. Optional gearboxes included a close-ratio four-speed and the FMX automatic. The GT-500 retained the fire-breathing 428-cid Cobra Jet V-8 from the previous year. A close-ratio four-speed was standard, with the C-6 back as an optional automatic.

Modifications to the 1969 Shelby suspension were minimal and included heavy-duty Mustang components from the Ford factory. Staggered shocks were standard on the GT-500 in order to control the rear axle during occasional hard launches. Gone were the stamped steel wheels, replaced with a five-spoke, 15 x 7-inch rim that mounted Goodyear belted E-70 x 15 wide oval tires (F-60x15 tires were optional).

Some Shelbys wound up with Boss 302 "Magnum 500" wheels when a defect was discovered in the stock rim, forcing a recall.

Carroll Shelby convinced Ford to end the GT-350/500 program in the fall of 1969 because the American auto industry and federal government were tightening the screws on performance cars. Also, Ford Motor Company was mass-producing cars that competed directly, such as the Mach 1, Boss 302, and Boss 429. Sales for 1969 were 1,087 GT-350 fastbacks, 194 GT-350 convertibles, 1,534 GT-500 fastbacks and 335 GT-500 convertibles.

Shelby agreed to update 1969 leftovers into 1970 models with new vehicle identification numbers, a set of black hood stripes, a chin spoiler, and an emissions control unit required for that year. There is no accurate count of how many 1970 Shelbys were created. Some reports say 789 units finished off the 1969 carryovers.

1970 MUSTANG MACH 1

1970 MUSTANG

Improvements to the 1970 Mustang were limited to subtle cosmetic changes to the Mustang's front and rear and the dropping of the big-block 390 engine. Two round headlamps located inside a wider grille opening were flanked by simulated air intakes and the tail lamp housing was slightly restyled. Gone were the side-mounted fake air intakes. The side fender-mounted reflector grew larger for 1970 and became a vertical strip above the bumper line.

Updates to the popular Mach 1 included a flat panel with honeycomb trim between the tail lamps and ribbed aluminum rocker panel moldings (with big Mach 1 call-outs). A black-striped hood with standard fake scoop replaced the 1969 matte-black hood. Optional hood clips from 1969 were replaced with new twist-in pins and the Shaker hood scoop was available with the 351 V-8. The steering wheel changed from 1969 three-spoke classic look to a more mundane two-spoke design. A larger rear stripe, larger rear call-out, mag-type hubcaps, wide 14x7-inch wheels, and bright oval exhaust tips were also new. Black-painted styled wheels were a no-cost option.

The Boss 302 and 429 were largely unchanged in their second and final year of production.

The good news for 1970 Mustang fans is that Ford captured the Trans-Am title that year, just as the company was officially ending its competition program. The bad news is with competition from the Dodge Challenger, plus redesigned Barracudas, Camaros and Firebirds, the Mustang lost around 100,000 sales in 1970. A total of 190,727 1970 Mustangs were built.

Bunkie Knudsen's short reign over Ford ended in August of 1969 when Chairman Henry Ford II fired him.

1970 Production Chart

Model	Price	Weight	Production
01 (hardtop)	$2,721	2,721	82,569
01 (hardtop Grandé)	$2,926	2,806	13,581
02 (fastback)	$2,771	2,745	45,934
02 (fastback Mach 1)	$3,271	3,240	40,970
03 (convertible)	$3,025	2,831	7,673
Year Total			190,727

1970 MUSTANG TWISTER SPECIAL

1970 TWISTER SPECIAL

Because there was a time in the 1960s when Ford Motor Co. rewarded certain dealers or regions for their high sales numbers, we have today a dozen or more collectible Mustangs designed for certain areas of the country. The 1968 California Special was one such unusual model, perhaps the best known because so many were built for such a high-profile state. Other obvious entries in the field would be the various pace car replicas built for the Indy 500, Texas International Speedway and other competition events.

In 1969 representatives of the Kansas City sales district requested Ford to produce a special run of pace/feature cars for a promotional event at the Kansas City International Raceway. Fortunately for the dealers, Ford had designed a batch of 1970 Mustang pace cars to be used at five racetracks owned by American Raceways Inc. just before that company declared bankruptcy. With Mustangs already in the pipeline, the KC request was quickly satisfied with 96

Twister Special Mach 1s painted Grabber Orange. A shortage of big-block engines diluted the dealer request for all cars to be equipped with 428 SCJs though and half of the orders were filled with 351s.

Like most promotional Mustangs, the Twisters were displayed during the November 7 event, then sold to the public with their commemorative graphics still in place.

1970 Engines				
Code	Engine	Intake	Power (hp)	Transmission
T	200-cid 6	1-bbl	115	M3, A3
L	250-cid 6	1-bbl	155	M3, A3
F	302-cid V-8	2-bbl	220	M3, M4, A3
G (Boss)	302-cid V-8	4-bbl	290	M4
H	351-cid V-8	2-bbl	250	M3, M4, A3
M	351-cid V-8	4-bbl	300	M3, M4, A3
Q (CJ)	428-cid V-8	4-bbl	335	M4, A3
R (SCJ)	428-cid V-8	4-bbl	360	M4, A3
Z (Boss)	429-cid V-8	4-bbl	375	M4

1970 BOSS 429

1970 BOSS 302 AND 429

The Boss 302 package continued with minor changes for 1970, including the stock Mustang's revised front and rear styling, new Grabber paint colors, and a "hockey stick" striping treatment with the name "Boss 302" above and on the "blade" on the upper front fender. Wide 15 x 7-inch steel wheels with hubcaps and trim rings were standard, while the shaker hood became an option. High-back bucket seats were added to the standard features list. Smaller diameter valves and a new crankshaft were used in the small-block performance V-8 and most Boss 302s received finned aluminum valve covers. A rear sway bar was added to the suspension and the front one was thickened.

In its January 1970 edition, *Hot Rod* reported the new Boss was "definitely the best handling car Ford has ever built." Motor Trend called the Boss Mustang, "The word of our time. Good, only better, fuller, rounder and more intense." It was praise that put the car above competitors GTO, Road Runner and Chevelle. Not surprisingly, the practical-thinking Consumer Guide labeled it "...uncomfortable at any speed over anything but the smoothest surface."

Unfortunately for performance fans, the passing of the Boss 302 at the end of 1970 marked the end of the high-compression, high-revving Detroit muscle cars.

1970 Boss 302/ 429 Production Chart

Model	Price	Weight	Production
02 (fastback Boss 302)	$3,720	3,250	7,014
02 (fastback Boss 429)	$3,979	3,530	499
Year Total			7,513

1970 Boss 302/ 429 Engines

Code	Engine	Power (hp)	Transmission
G	302-cid V-8	290	M4
Z	429-cid V-8	375	M4

1971 MUSTANG HARDTOP

1971 MUSTANG

For 1971, the Mustang just kept getting bigger in every way compared to the 1970 model. It gained 1.0 inch in the wheelbase (to 109 inches), 2.1 inches of length (189.5) and 500 lbs. — but the design left no doubt about the car's heritage. The original long hood/short deck proportions remained, and there were clearly some evolutionary steps taken between 1965 and 1971, including a nearly horizontal fastback roof and the recessed rear window featured on the coupes.

After a two-year absence, the corral protecting a chrome pony returned to the center of the grille on standard models. An optional grille deleted the corral, but offered amber auxiliary lights imbedded in the honeycomb-textured surface; on these models, the galloping horse was depicted on a small tri-bar emblem in the grille's center. A chrome bumper and chrome fender and hood moldings were standard, except on Mach 1's and Boss 351s.

Model distinctions were the same as the '70 model: hardtop, SportsRoof and convertible. The Grandé, Mach 1, and Boss models returned. A new Boss 351 replaced the Boss 302 and Boss 429. Its 330-hp 351-cid Cleveland engine became the Mustang's small-block, high-performance V-8.

Timing was not friendly to the new Mustang, which had been designed around powerful big-block V-8s in a time of limitless cheap gasoline, but built during America's transition to environmental responsibility. Ford's desire to turn the Mustang into both a super car platform and a luxurious and spacious daily driver for sporty young families bloated the package to the point that it was nearly indistinguishable from the company's other mid-size offerings.

Mustang production for 1971 continued to decline, dropping to 149,678.

1971 Production Chart			
Model	**Price**	**Weight**	**Production**
01 (hardtop)	$2,911	2,937	65,696
02 (fastback)	$2,973	2,907	23,956
03 (convertible)	$3,227	3,059	6,121
04 (hardtop Grandé)	$3,117	2,963	17,406
05 (fastback Mach 1)	$3,268	3,220	36,449
Year Total			149,678

1971 MUSTANG MACH 1 WITH 429SCJ V-8

1971 MUSTANG MACH 1

For 1971, Mach 1's received the standard SportsRoof equipment, plus a color-keyed spoiler/bumper with color-keyed hood and front fender moldings. Also color-keyed were the dual racing mirrors, with the left-hand mirror featuring remote-control operation. Mach 1s came standard with the sport lamp grille; com-petition suspension; hubcaps and trim rings; a black, honeycomb-textured back panel appli-qué; a pop-open gas cap; a deck lid paint stripe; black or argent silver lower body side finish with bright moldings at the upper edge; E70-14 whitewalls; and the base V-8. NASA-style hood scoops were optional at no extra charge.

1971 Engines				
Code	**Engine**	**Intake**	**Power (hp)**	**Transmission**
L	250-cid 6	1-bbl	145	M3, A3
F	302-cid V-8	2-bbl	210	M3, A3
H	351-cid V-8	2-bbl	240	M3, A3
M (to 5/71)	351-cid V-8	4-bbl	285	M4, A3
M (CJ)	351-cid V-8	4-bbl	280	M4, A3
R (Boss)	351-cid V-8	4-bbl	330	M4
C (CJ)	429-cid V-8	4-bbl	370	M4
J (SCJ)	429-cid V-8	4-bbl	375	M4

1971 429-CID V-8

429-CID V-8 ENGINE

The 1971 Mustang's big body would have been too heavy for the small 200-cid inline six-cylinder to pull. In its place at the bottom of the power plant list was a slightly more powerful 250-cid six. A mild, 210-hp/302-cid engine was the standard V-8 for the line, with other small-block offerings including 240- and 285-hp versions of the 351-cid V-8, plus the Boss 351 engine.

The new 429 Cobra Jet (429CJ) engine sold for $372 more than the cost of the base V-8, and a 429 Cobra Jet Ram Air (429CJ-R) option was $436 above the base V-8, both rated at 370 hp. A 429 Super Cobra Jet with Dual Ram Air induction and a 375 hp rating was available for $531 over the base V-8. Hydraulic valve lifters, four-bolt main caps, dress-up aluminum valve covers and a GM Quadrajet four-barrel carburetor were part of the 429CJ-R performance package. The 429SCJ-R featured mechanical lifters, adjustable rocker arms, a larger Holley four-barrel carburetor, and forged pistons.

Ordering a 429CJ-R engine gave the buyer a competition suspension; Mach 1 hood; 80-ampere battery; 55-ampere alternator; dual exhausts; extra-cooling package; bright engine dress-up kit with cast aluminum rocker covers and a 3.25:1 ratio, non-locking rear axle. It was not available with air conditioning combined with the Drag Pak option or with the Dual Ram induction option. A C-6 Cruise-O-Matic or close-ratio four-speed manual transmission was required, along with disc brakes. Power steering was required on air-conditioned cars. The 429SCJ engine required the Drag Pak option and a 3.91:1 or 4.11:1 high-ratio rear axle.

The 1971 429 V-8 was not related to the Boss 429 power plant, which was derived from Ford's NASCAR "semi-hemi" design. It was actually built on a 460-cid Thunderbird/Lincoln block destroked to 429 cubic inches and topped with "wedge" heads.

About 1,250 Mustangs were built with 429 Cobra Jet and Super Cobra Jet V-8s — the last big-block Mustangs ever built.

1971 BOSS 351

1971 BOSS 351

Rather than create small- and big-block super cars as it had produced in 1969 and '70, Ford built its fastest 1971 model around a 351-cid V-8. Although installed in a bigger, heavier car, the Boss 351 engine was a strong performer, featuring solid lifters, four-bolt mains, large port cylinder heads and valves, 11.7:1 compression and aluminum valve covers. The Boss 351 was rated at 330 hp.

The Boss' standard equipment included all of the Mustang basics, plus a functional NASA-style hood with Black or Argent Silver full hood paint treatment, hood lock pins, and Ram Air engine decals. Also featured were racing mirrors; black or argent silver body side tape stripes (these also became optional on Mach 1s late in the year); color-keyed hood and front fender moldings; Boss 351 nomenclature; dual exhausts; power front disc brakes; a competition suspension with staggered rear shocks;

and a 3.91:1 axle ratio with Traction-Lok differential. A functional black spoiler was shipped "knocked-down" inside the car for dealer installation. The Boss also had an electronic rpm-limiter; a special cooling package; a wide-ratio four-speed manual transmission with Hurst shifter; and the 351-cid H.O. (high-output) V-8 with 330 hp. A chrome bumper was standard on Boss 351s, while the Mach 1-style color-keyed bumper was an option.

Comparing a 429 CJ Mach 1 to a Boss 351, *Sports Car Graphic* magazine declared the big-block car to be only marginally faster, with a zero-to-60 time of 6.3 seconds versus the Boss' 6.6. The 429 pulled the big pony through the quarter-mile in 14.6 seconds at 99.4 miles per hour, while the small-block managed 14.7 seconds and 96.2 miles per hour.

Ford discontinued the Boss 351 in the middle of the model year after 1,806 units were sold.

1971 Boss 351 Production Chart			
Model	**Price**	**Weight**	**Production**
02 (fastback Boss 351)	$4,124	3,123	1,806

1971 Boss 351 Engine			
Code	**Engine**	**Power (hp)**	**Transmission**
R	351-cid V-8	330	M4

1972 MUSTANG SPRINT CONVERTIBLE

1972 MUSTANG

Not surprisingly, the 1972 Mustang changed very little, with models including the hardtop, SportsRoof, convertible, Grandé and Mach 1. The Boss 351 did not return. Buyers had the choice of two distinct grille treatments depending on which boxes were checked on the options list. Bumpers could be either chromed or painted body color. Base models sported cursive "Mustang" lettering on the far right of the deck lid overhang. The Mach 1 received a decal instead of a badge.

Patriotic fervor swept through Ford in 1972 as the company released a series of red, white, and blue color schemes on its Mustangs, Maver-icks, and Pinto Runabouts. Although Ford dealers were limited to fastbacks and hardtops when ordering this Sprint Decor option, 50 convertibles were built for use in the Washington, D.C., Cherry Blossom Day parade.

Three 351-cid V-8s of were optional in Mustangs — the regular two-barrel version, the regular four-barrel version, and the four-barrel H.O. option offering 168, 200, and 275 hp, respectively.

If all the 1972 engine output figures seem like a massive drop from 1971 horsepower ratings, it's because the new numbers were expressed in SAE net horsepower.

1972 Production Chart

Model	Price	Weight	Production
01 (hardtop)	$2,729	2,941	57,350
02 (fastback)	$2,786	2,909	15,622
03 (convertible)	$3,015	3,061	6,401
04 (hardtop Grandé)	$2,915	2,965	18,045
05 (fastback Mach 1)	$3,053	3,046	27,675
Year Total			125,093

1972 Engines

Code	Engine	Intake	Power (hp)	Transmission
L	250-cid 6	1-bbl	98	M3, A3
F	302-cid V-8	2-bbl	140	M3, A3
H	351-cid V-8	2-bbl	168	M3, A3
Q (CJ)	351-cid V-8	4-bbl	200	M4, A3
R (HO)	351-cid V-8	4-bbl	275	M4

1973 MUSTANG HARDTOP

1973 MUSTANG HARDTOP

For the first time in the Mustang's history, Ford did not stick to a schedule of two-year model introductions. The 1973 cars were marketed with only minor cosmetic and mechanical changes. In order to meet federal safety regulations and smog guidelines, the new Mustang suffered another weight and size increase, largely because of a new impact-resistant front bumper. The color-keyed bumper extended the overall length of the Mustang by another four inches, to a whopping 194! A new crosshatch-design grille, featuring a floating pony badge at the center (or tri-bar emblem on sportier models) and an egg crate-style insert with vertical parking lights in the outboard segments gave the 1973 model a mild facelift.

The standard equipment list included a 250-cid six or 302-cid V-8 base engine; E78-14 bias-belted black sidewall tires; a lower back panel appliqué with a bright molding; all-vinyl upholstery and door trim; a front mini-console; and a deluxe two-spoke steering wheel with wood-tone insert. SportsRoof models received a tinted back window and fixed rear quarter windows. Convertibles also had under-dash courtesy lamps, a power-operated convertible top, a color-keyed top boot, a glass backlight, ComfortWeave knit-vinyl seat trim and power front disc brakes.

Ordering the luxury hardtop Grandé gave buyers color-keyed dual racing mirrors; a vinyl roof; body side tape striping; special wheel covers; Lambeth cloth and vinyl seat trim; molded door panels with integral arm rests; bright pedal pads; a deluxe instrument panel and an electric clock.

Some safety refinements were made to the instrument panel, primarily to eliminate protruding objects and glare. Larger brakes were used, too. New, flame-retardant interior fabrics were required and the emissions system also received some attention. Engine choices were virtually identical to 1972, with the exception of the dropped 351 H.O.

In its final year, the big Mustang saw a jump in sales, owing largely to Ford's news that 1973 would be its last year of convertible production (convertible sales doubled to more than 11,000). When it was all said and done, the count stood at 134,817 units for the model year.

1973 MUSTANG MACH 1

1973 MUSTANG MACH 1

The Mach 1 took on a new body side stripe scheme that relocated the model name to just behind the door edge. Standard equipment for the Mach 1 included a 302-cid/140-hp V-8; competition suspension; choice of a NASA- or plain-style hood; E70-14 whitewall Wide-Oval tires; color-keyed dual racing mirrors; black grille; black back panel appliqué; hubcaps with wheel trim rings; tinted back window; all-vinyl upholstery and door trim; and high-back front bucket seats.

Mach 1 buyers had the option of adding a two-barrel or four-barrel version of the 351 V-8. Only the two-barrel version, rated at 177 horsepower, was available with a functional Ram Air induction system.

1973 Production Chart

Model	Price	Weight	Production
01 (hardtop)	$2,760	2,984	51,430
02 (fastback)	$2,820	2,991	10,820
03 (convertible)	$3,102	3,106	11,853
04 (hardtop Grandé)	$2,946	2,982	25,274
05 (fastback Mach 1)	$3,088	3,090	35,440
Year Total			125,093

1973 Engines

Code	Engine	Intake	Power (hp)	Transmission
L	250-cid 6	1-bbl	98	M3, A3
F	302-cid V-8	2-bbl	140	M3, A3
H	351-cid V-8	2-bbl	177	A3
Q (CJ)	351-cid V-8	4-bbl	248	M4, A3

1973 SLOTTED MAG WHEEL

ALLOY WHEELS

Even though engine performance and development seemed to be on a decline with Ford in 1973, the company was finally bringing to market some modern wheel and tire technologies.

Ford replaced the long-in-the-tooth Magnum 500 wheel in 1973 with a fresh dish-type, five-slot design made of lightweight forged aluminum. This optional 14-inch rim (that cost an additional $111 on the Mach 1, $119 on the Grandé, and $142 on other models) established a fashionably sporty look that would carry through the final Mustang II in 1978.

Ordering a set of new steel-belted radial ply tires to go on those wheels greatly improved the big Mustang's handling characteristics.

1974 MUSTANG II HARDTOP

1974 MUSTANG II

The Mustang II looked like a 1973 Mustang shrunk down by a mad scientist's experiment. Its 96.2-inch wheelbase was 11.8 inches less than the 1965 Mustang and more than a foot down from the 1973 wheelbase. Though changed more than ever before, the basic Mustang image and long hood/short deck proportions were still preserved in the new car, although it had many modern touches.

After much debate and consumer clinic review, marketers decided to offer both a hardtop and fastback body style and their upscale derivatives, the Ghia and performance-oriented Mach 1.

Base prices for 1974 Mustang IIs ran from $3,081 to $3,621, although optional equipment and packages had many shoppers gasping to find stickers reading well over $4,500. Ford kept production costs to the bare minimum by spinning the new car from an existing model. The Pinto was the base vehicle, with which the Mustang II shared some components (although fewer than its detractors would claim). To Ford's credit, many of those components were upgraded and installed in keeping with the more-expensive Mustang.

Promoting the car as a luxury model backfired, but the II quickly found its real niche as an economy car, and IIs were shipped to dealers with fewer options. Viewed in this light, and considering the impact of the 1973 OPEC oil embargo, its timing was perfect. Ford advertised it as "the right car at the right time" — a slogan that proved more truthful than the company first thought. The low-end hardtop and 2+2 accounted for 252,470 of all first-year Mustang IIs produced.

1974 Production Chart			
Model	**Price**	**Weight**	**Production**
02 (hardtop)	$3,081	2,620	177,671
03 (hatchback)	$3,275	2,699	74,799
04 (coupe Ghia)	$3,427	2,866	89,477
05 (hatchback Mach 1)	$3,621	2,778	44,046
Year Total			385,993

1974 MUSTANG II 2.3-LITER FOUR

1974 MUSTANG II POWERTRAINS

As further argument that the Mustang II shared nothing with its predecessors, the powertrain lineup was entirely new for 1974. Enthusiasts could no longer order big-block V-8s as they had from 1967 through 1971. In fact, there were no V-8 engines planned for the II series, just metric-measured four-cylinder engines and German-built V-6s.

The Mustang II's standard engine was a 2.3-liter "Lima" four (named for its production plant in Ohio) equipped with a single overhead camshaft and power that compared favorably to Ford's heavier and much older 200-cid inline six-cylinder. Like every Mustang II component, the engine was subjected to intense research and development to meet high noise, vibration, and harshness (NVH) standards. Service-free hydraulic valve-lash adjusters were unique for any overhead cam four-cylinder and made the engine especially attractive to the II's target market, for whom trouble-free operation was a priority. Major emissions equipment was designed into the engine. Metric measurement meant the Lima could share components from around the world, a benefit for future model development. The four-cylinder engine could pull the Mustang II 23 miles on a gallon of gas, considered quite economical for an American car at that time.

Ford of Germany contributed its 2.8-liter V-6, an engine proven in the sporty Mercury Capri, to the Mustang II lineup. The 2.8 was rated at 105 horsepower but brought with it many mechanical headaches. Problems with engine valves, piston rings, and the cooling system were typical. The V-6 was available only with the four-speed manual transmission, but the four-cylinder could be purchased with either manual or three-speed SelectShift automatic.

With a V-8, sales would probably have gone even higher. By the time 1975 models bowed Ford had rectified this misstep.

1974 Engines				
Code	Engine	Intake	Power (hp)	Transmission
Y	140-cid SOHC 4	2-bbl	88	M4, A3
Z	171-cid V-6	2-bbl	105	M4

1975 MUSTANG II 5.0-LITER V-8

1975 5.0-LITER V-8

The 1975 Mustang II incorporated several modifications and improvements that went unnoticed by casual fans. The most obvious change in the lineup was the return of the 302-cid (5.0-liter) V-8. To shoehorn the larger engine into such a small space, a longer hood, repositioned radiator, new mounts for the plastic grille and new No. 2 cross member were necessary.

Base hardtop and fastback buyers could add the V-8 option for $199; Mach 1 owners got it for $172. The 122-hp two-barrel engine was often described as "thirsty," as it got only 13.7 to 15.9 miles per gallon. It could move the Mustang II along at 105 mph — adequate for the time period — and sent it down the quarter-mile in 17.9 seconds at 77 mph. The midyear introduction of an MPG package, when teamed with a 3.18:1 rear axle, reportedly produced 30-plus miles per gallon.

All V-8 Mustang IIs sold in 1975 were equipped with SelectShift automatic transmissions. V-6 engines were only linked to four-speed manuals.

After the V-8, probably the most exciting news for the II was the availability of a manually operated sunroof option. Ford saw production of the 1975 Mustang II taper off to 188,575 cars, or 2.88 percent of the industry total.

1975 Production Chart			
Model	**Price**	**Weight**	**Production**
02 (hardtop)	$3,529	2,660	85,155
03 (hatchback)	$3,818	2,697	30,038
04 (coupe Ghia)	$3,938	2,704	52,320
05 (hatchback Mach 1)	$4,188	2,879	21,062
Year Total			185,575

1975 Engines				
Code	**Engine**	**Intake**	**Power (hp)**	**Transmission**
Y	140-cid SOHC 4	2-bbl	88	M4, A3
Z	171-cid V-6	2-bbl	105	M4
F	302-cid V-8	2-bbl	122	A3

1976 MUSTANG II

1976 MUSTANG II

All base Mustang II models, hardtops or hatchbacks, were known as "MPGs" in 1976, a designation indicating a lower 2.79:1 axle ratio and optional wide-ratio manual transmission. The smaller Mustang II engines were robbed of some power, with the four going from 97 to 92 hp and the V-6 dropping from 105 to 103 hp. However, the V-8 got a substantial boost from 122 to 139 hp.

Ghia upgrades were basically the same as before, although the stand-up hood ornament was no longer standard. It became part of the Luxury Group option. The Mach 1 (official name: "Mustang II Mach 1 2+2 3-door") also had the same add-ons as before. Strangely, since the V-6 engine was standard in the Mach 1, that model could not be had in MPG trim.

With sales of 187,567 Mustang IIs in 1976, Lee Iacocca's "little jewel" dominated the domestic subcompact sporty car market in its third year. Improvements in fuel economy at a time when the nation was still skittish about buying more gas guzzlers, and a few enhancements such as stalk-mounted windshield wiper controls (first seen mid-1975) kept the II on a path of slow but steady evolution.

1976 Production Chart			
Model	**Price**	**Weight**	**Production**
02 (hardtop)	$3,525	2,678	78,508
03 (hatchback)	$3,781	2,706	62,312
04 (coupe Ghia)	$3,859	2,729	37,515
05 (hatchback Mach 1)	$4,209	2,822	9,232
Year Total			187,567

1976 MUSTANG II COBRA II

1976 MUSTANG II COBRA II

Enhancing the Mustang II's image in 1976 was the new Cobra II package, a hatchback-only model with the look of a Shelby Mustang. Carroll Shelby's presence in magazine ads touted the option.

"Cobra strikes again," said the Free Wheelin' catalog (a youth-oriented, 24-page color booklet and probably one of the sexiest pieces of factory literature Ford ever produced). "New Cobra II. Ford's Mustang II wrapped in an appearance package that does justice to the Cobra name. So striking, it's already a sales success." The Cobra II was on its way to reaching an approving audience, since the package was available on all 2+2s with any engine.

The new Cobra was an appearance-only package. A base hatchback started with Mustang II MPG standard equipment like rack and pinion steering; front disc brakes; and the 2.3-liter four-cylinder, two-barrel engine (for added punch, the V-6 or V-8 could be added). The following special Cobra II equipment was added: bold racing stripes; a black grille; racing mirrors; rear quarter window louvers; a front air dam; a non-functional hood scoop; a rear deck lid spoiler; a brushed aluminum instrument panel and door panel appliqués; Cobra insignias on the front fenders; styled steel wheels and BR70 steel-belted tires with raised white letters. The $325 1976 Cobra II option came in white with blue stripes, blue with white stripes, or black with gold stripes.

Jim Wangers, who fathered the Pontiac GTO, was responsible for designing and installing the Cobra II-unique graphics and aerodynamic pieces at a small plant near the Dearborn Ford factory. His company, Motortown, produced all Cobra IIs for 1976. Ford took the popular package in-house for 1977 and 1978.

1976 Production Chart				
Code	Engine	Intake	Power (hp)	Transmission
Y	140-cid SOHC 4	2-bbl	92	M4, A3
Z	171-cid V-6	2-bbl	103	M4, A3
F	302-cid V-8	2-bbl	139	M4, A3

1977 MUSTANG II COBRA II

1977 MUSTANG II

There were few changes in the Mustang II for 1977, although the four and the V-6 both lost a few more horsepower as emission upgrades continued to choke off engine performance. The V-8 retained its 139-hp rating, but California models received a variable-venturi carburetor. Buyers in that state were also limited to four-cylinder Mustang IIs or V-8 cars with automatic transmissions.

Joining the option list were simulated wire wheel covers; painted cast aluminum spoke wheels; a flip-up removable sunroof; four-way manual bucket seats and high-altitude option. On the all-new twin-panel T-roof option, a wide black band ran across the top (except with the Cobra II).

The optional Cobra II package climbed more than $220 in price, to $535. Cobras built early in the year had Cobra II lettering low on the doors. Later cars had much larger lettering that ran higher up on the doors.

1977 Production Chart			
Model	**Price**	**Weight**	**Production**
02 (hardtop)	$3,702	2,627	67,783
03 (hatchback)	$3,901	2,672	49,161
04 (coupe Ghia)	$4,119	2,667	29,510
05 (hatchback Mach 1)	$4,332	2,785	6,719
Year Total			153,173*

*Totals shown include 20,937 Mustangs produced as 1978 models but sold as 1977 models (9,826 notchbacks, 7,019 hatchbacks, 3,209 Ghias, and 883 Mach 1s) due to a problem meeting emissions regulations.

1977 Engines				
Code	**Engine**	**Intake**	**Power (hp)**	**Transmission**
Y	140-cid SOHC 4	2-bbl	89	M4, A3
Z	171-cid V-6	2-bbl	93	M4, A3
F	302-cid V-8	2-bbl	139	M4, A3

1978 MUSTANG II COBRA II

1978 MUSTANG II

In its final year of production before the all-new 1979 model, the Mustang II still reigned supreme over its competitors in the domestic sporty subcompact class.

For the third year in a row, more power was robbed from the base four (now rated at 88 hp) and the optional V-6 (down to 90 hp). The V-8 was again credited with the same 139 hp. The SelectShift Cruise-O-Matic transmission cost $225 extra with V-8s and $263 in other models.

The Mach 1, a proven sales success, returned again with the 2.8-liter V-6, styled wheels and raised white-letter tires, plus black front and rear bumpers and lower body side paint. A brushed aluminum instrument panel appliqué and full instrumentation added to its youthful appeal.

A fun-to-own, fun-to-drive car, the Cobra II carried on in the form introduced at mid-year in 1977. Tri-color tape stripes decorated body sides and front spoiler, front bumper, hood, hood scoop, roof, deck lid and rear spoiler. Huge "Cobra" block letters went on the center body side tape stripe and deck lid spoiler, a Cobra decal appeared on the back spoiler, and a

Cobra II snake emblem sat on the black grille. The package also included black quarter-window and backlight louvers, black rocker panels, dual racing mirrors, and a rear-opening hood scoop.

A Fashion Accessory Group, included a four-way adjustable driver's seat, striped cloth seat inserts, illuminated entry, and a lighted driver's vanity visor mirror. It came in nine body colors.

Model year production leaped to 192,410 units in the Mustang II's final season. V-8 engines were optionally installed in 17.9 percent of the Mustang IIs.

1978 Production Chart

Model	Price	Weight	Production
02 (hardtop)	$3,555	2,608	81,304
03 (hatchback)	$3,798	2,654	68,408
04 (coupe Ghia)	$3,972	2,646	34,730
05 (hatchback Mach 1)	$4,253	2,733	7,968
Year Total			192,410 *

*Totals shown do not include 20,937 Mustangs produced as 1978 models, but sold as 1977 models.

1978 MUSTANG II KING COBRA

1978 MUSTANG II KING COBRA

The new "Boss of the Mustang Stable" is how Ford described its single-year King Cobra.

The package might be viewed as a regular Cobra and more of the same, with plenty of striping and lettering. The King did without the customary body side striping, but sported a unique tape treatment including a giant snake decal on the hood and pinstriping on the greenhouse, deck lid, wheel lips, rocker panels, belt, over-the-roof area, and around the side windows. Up front was a tough-looking spoiler.

The 302-cid (5.0-liter) V-8 was standard on the King, along with a four-speed transmission and power brakes and power steering. A "King Cobra" nameplate went on each door and the back spoiler and a "5.0L" badge appeared on the front hood scoop. The King Cobra also had rear quarter flares, a black grille and moldings, and color-keyed dual sport mirrors.

Raised-white-letter tires rode lacy-spoke aluminum wheels with twin rings and a Cobra symbol on the hubs. Only 4,318 buyers paid the extra $1,277 for the King Cobra package.

1978 Engines				
Code	Engine	Intake	Power (hp)	Transmission
Y	140-cid SOHC 4	2-bbl	88	M4, A3
Z	171-cid V-6	2-bbl	90	M4, A3
F	302-cid V-8	2-bbl	139	M4, A3

1979 MUSTANG HARDTOP

1979 MUSTANG

With the introduction of the all-new, 1979 Mustang, Ford announced to the world that America's favorite pony car was facing a bright and, literally, turbocharged future. The "new breed" third-generation offered a chance to boost the marque's image. Ready for the 1980s, the Mustang offered a pleasing blend of American and European design.

Detroit learned that incorporating basic principles of aviation science into passenger car design could pay off in big ways. A vehicle designed more like a drop of water can cheat the wind. In production trim, the new pony car set a milestone for Ford by registering a slippery 0.44 coefficient of drag for the fastback and 0.46 for the notchback.

The aerodynamic wedge design featured a sloping front and hood, and a sculpted roofline. A lowered window line gave the Mustang large glass area for improved visibility. As in the prior version, two-door notchback and three-door hatchback bodies were offered in base and Ghia levels.

The new model's diet of advanced plastics, aluminum, high-strength/low-alloy steel, thinner but stronger glass, and slimmer passenger compartment components made it 200 lbs. lighter than the previous year's smaller Mustang II. Fastback and notchback both registered in the 2,600-lb. range. Specs for the new pony included a 100.4-inch wheelbase, an overall length of 179.1 inches and a body width of 69.1 inches. Interior space was increased by more than 20 percent.

A V-8 powered hatchback was selected to pace the 63rd annual Indianapolis 500 on May 27, 1979, and replicas were available through Ford dealerships.

1979 Production Chart			
Model	**Price**	**Weight**	**Production**
02 (hardtop)	$4,071	2,431	156,666
03 (hatchback)	$4,436	2,451	120,535
04 (coupe Ghia)	$4,642	2,539	56,351
05 (hatchback Ghia)	$4,824	2,548	36,384
Year Total			369,936

1979 MUSTANG INDY PACE CAR

1979 TURBO FOUR

Most customers attracted to the fresh new 1979 design were able to ignore the fact that the engines — the 2.3-liter four-cylinder; 2.8-liter V-6; and 5.0-liter V-8 — were essentially Mustang II carryovers. (The V-6 was offered initially, until a supply problem forced Ford to substitute its ancient 200-cid inline six-cylinder.)

Accompanying the forward-look sheet metal was the engine of the future–at least as far as Ford marketers were concerned at the time—an optional turbocharged version of the 2.3-liter four rated at 131 hp. According to Ford, the blown four offered "V-8 performance without sacrificing fuel economy" with company test results indicating the Mustang turbo could zip from zero to 55 miles an hour in just over 8 seconds (a little quicker than a V-8).

Ford had gone to market too soon with its turbocharged engine and buyers suffered for it. Slapping a Garrett AiResearch TO-3 turbo-charger onto the underperforming 2.3-liter and two-barrel carburetor created some serious reliability issues, such as burned-out turbines and fatal oil leaks.

Ford withdrew its Turbo Four from the market at the end of 1980, although advertising for 1981 Mustangs suggests it was still available. The company released a more reliable and powerful turbo package in the middle of the 1983 model year. It would prove unpopular with customers and disappeared in 1986.

1979 Engines				
Code	Engine	Intake	Power (hp)	Transmission
Y	140-cid SOHC 4	2-bbl	88	M4, A3
W	140-cid SOHC 4 T	2-bbl	131	M4, A3
Z	171-cid V-6	2-bbl	109	M4, A3
T	200-cid 6	1-bbl	85	M4, A3
F	302-cid V-8	2-bbl	140	M4, A3

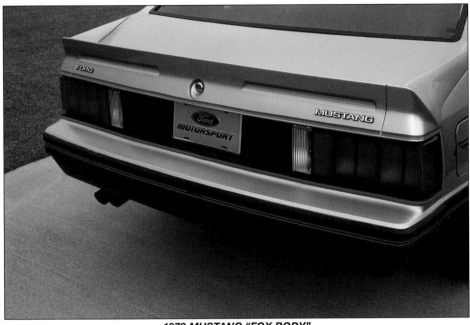

1979 MUSTANG "FOX BODY"

"FOX" MUSTANG

As is its habit, Ford built the 1979 Mustang around a platform it would share with more humble cars in the Lincoln-Mercury-Ford corporate family in order to keep development and construction costs down. Deep beneath the new pony's distinctive sheet metal was Ford Fairmont and Mercury Zephyr DNA in the form of the "Fox" unit-body platform.

When introduced in 1979, no one had any idea the Fox-body Mustang would be in production for the next 26 years! Upgrades and evolutionary steps occurred during that time, of course, such as the transition Ford made to the "Fox-4" chassis in 1994, but very few automotive designs have survived and flourished for such a long period.

Ford referred to its new Mustang's chassis by that name because the company used as its engineering target the just-released Audi/Volkswagen Fox. At least 25 different vehicles would be built on the Fox platform, including the Capri, Granada/Versailles, Thunderbird/Cougar and Lincoln Continental.

All Fox parts were purged from the Mustang with the 2005 introduction of the S197 platform.

MICHELIN TRX WHEEL/TIRE PACKAGE

TRX WHEEL/TIRE OPTION

Unlike during the Mustang II era, performance packages actually contributed to the 1979 car's thrill-behind-the-wheel quotient.

Two such packages were offered that year. The basic handling suspension option with 14-inch radial tires included different spring rates and shock valving, stiffer bushings in the front suspension and upper arm in the rear, plus a special rear stabilizer bar. The second level package came with a Michelin TRX tire option, featuring ultra-low aspect ratio tires introduced on Ford's European Granada.

The TRX's 15.35-inch (390mm) size demanded special metric wheels. That package also included unique shock valving, increased spring rates, and wider front and rear stabilizer bars.

When the off-size TRX package was announced General Motors, in what many considered a fit of corporate jealousy, filed a complaint with the Department of Transportation to keep the high-performance Michelins off the market, claiming factory workers could be injured if they attempted to mount the TRX on a regular wheel.

Mustang owners had to pay a premium when replacing the Michelin-specific tire but the package provided real improvements in handling while it was offered from 1979 through 1984. Today, restorers of early Fox-body Mustangs can find the TRX wheels for reasonable prices at swap meets, and the appropriate tires are still available.

1980 MUSTANG

1980 MUSTANG

Ford made very few modifications to the Fox-body Mustang in its second year. The base four-cylinder engine enjoyed a 23 percent fuel economy improvement, and there were only minor changes to the turbocharged version. The 200-cid straight six remained on the lineup after replacing the 2.8-liter V-6 at the end of 1979.

For the second time since it was introduced in 1968, the venerable 302-cid (5.0-liter) V-8 was dropped. In its place Ford put a de-bored 255-cid (4.2-liter) V-8 in an attempt to increase gas mileage for the fleet. Its 117 hp was 14 less than the lighter turbocharged four-cylinder. Both the non-turbocharged 2.3-liter four and in-line six could have a four-speed manual gearbox (overdrive fourth with the six), while all engines could be ordered with automatics.

All models now rode on high-pressure P-metric radial tires and benefited from halogen headlamps. Semi-metallic front disc brake pads were included with optional engines. A new Carriage Roof option for the notchback model was supposed to resemble a convertible, even though the car had a solid "B" pillar. It used diamond-grain vinyl. Other new options included a roof luggage rack, cargo area cover (hatchback), and Recaro adjustable seatback bucket seats.

1980 Production Chart

Model	Price	Weight	Production
02 (hardtop)	$4,884	2,497	128,893
03 (hatchback)	$5,194	2,531	98,497
04 (coupe Ghia)	$5,369	2,565	23,647
05 (hatchback Ghia)	$5,512	2,588	20,285
Year Total			271,322

1980 Engines

Code	Engine	Intake	Power (hp)	Transmission
A	140-cid SOHC 4	2-bbl	88	M4, A3
W	140-cid SOHC 4 T	2-bbl	150	M4, A3
B	200-cid 6	1-bbl	91	M4, A3
D	255-cid V-8	2-bbl	119	M4, A3

1981 MUSTANG COBRA

1981 MUSTANG

The 1981 Mustang was offered with the same limited array of powertrains — three optional engines and seven optional transmissions — with Ford dropping the unpopular turbocharged four-cylinder for reliability reasons. A five-speed manual overdrive gearbox was offered for the first time, initially on four-cylinder models, for an extra $152. Some critics found fault with the five-speed's shift pattern, which put fifth gear right next to fourth.

Also joining the option list was a T-Roof with twin removable tinted glass panels, offered on either the two-door notchback or three-door hatchback. The optional console included a graphic display module with built-in digital clock and warnings for low fuel or washer fluid level.

The $1,588 Cobra package was unchanged and included 190/65R-390 TRX tires on forged metric aluminum wheels, an 8000-rpm tachometer, "Cobra" tape treatment, hood scoop, sport-tuned exhaust, black bumper rub strips, body side moldings with dual accent stripes and black greenhouse moldings. The Cobra had a built-in front spoiler, black quarter-window louvers, model-unique medallion on dash and door trim and a handling suspension. 1981 was the final year for the Cobra cosmetic/performance option.

1981 Production Chart			
Model	**Price**	**Weight**	**Production**
10 (hardtop)	$6,171	2,524	77,458
15 (hatchback)	$6,408	2,544	77,399
12 (coupe Ghia)	$6,645	2,558	13,422
13 (hatchback Ghia)	$6,729	2,593	14,273
Year Total			182,552

1981 Engines				
Code	**Engine**	**Intake**	**Power (hp)**	**Transmission**
A	140-cid SOHC 4	2-bbl	88	M4, A3
B	200-cid 6	1-bbl	94	M4, A3
D	255-cid V-8	2-bbl	115	M4, A3

1982 MUSTANG GT

1982 MUSTANG GT

The biggest news of 1982 was the return of the 302-cid (5.0-liter) V-8 to the Mustang lineup. The 5.0-liter power plant, when teamed with a two-barrel carburetor, low-restriction air cleaner and four-speed transmission, is most often associated with the new GT model, although it could be installed in the entire Mustang line. It gener-ated 157 hp and recorded the fastest zero-to-60 mph time of any American car at the time.

Available in hatchback form only, the $8,308 GT was well positioned to capitalize on low gas prices. In its first year, V-8 installations rose to 25.5 percent of all Mustangs — about five times more than the number sold in 1981.

1982 Production Chart

Model	Price	Weight	Production
10 (hardtop L)	$6,345	2,511	*
10 (hardtop GL)	$6,844	2,528	45,316
16 (hatchback GL)	$6,979	2,565	69,348
12 (notchback GLX)	$6,980	2,543	5,828
13 (hatchback GLX)	$7,101	2,579	9,926
16 (hatchback GT)	$8,308	2,629	**
Year Total			130,418

*Production of L model is included in GL total.
**Ford figures include GT production in GL hatchback total above. Industry sources report a total of 23,447 GT models produced.

1982 Engines

Code	Engine	Intake	Power (hp)	Transmission
A	140-cid SOHC 4	2-bbl	86	M4, A3
B	200-cid 6	1-bbl	87	M4, A3
D	255-cid V-8	2-bbl	120	M4, A3
F	302-cid V-8	2-bbl	157	M4

1983 MUSTANG CONVERTIBLE

1983 MUSTANG

The base 2.3-liter four-cylinder was upgraded with a more efficient one-barrel carburetor and long-reach sparkplugs. The antique inline six-cylinder was replaced by a modern "Essex" 3.8-liter V-6 that cranked out 105 hp (versus the inline unit's 87 hp) with a two-barrel carburetor.

The 5.0 received a new four-barrel carburetor (the first such combo on a Mustang since 1970), an aluminum intake manifold, a high-flow air cleaner, and valve train mods, which pushed it to 175 horsepower. A Borg-Warner T5 close-ratio five-speed arrived later for the GT's high-output 5.0-liter V-8, hooked to a 3.27:1 final drive.

Another return to the Mustang lineup was the unlamented turbocharger option that had been dropped at the end of model year 1980. The 1983 power plant showed some real engineering savvy. Ford's development work promised more power, better reliability, and greater operating efficiency. The carburetor for Bosch port electronic fuel injection was eliminated and

the turbo was repositioned so it sat upstream of the induction system instead of downstream.

All Mustang tires increased by at least one size for 1983, while the optional handling suspension got thicker anti-sway bars plus springs and shocks tuned for sportier driving.

1983 Production Chart			
Model	**Price**	**Weight**	**Production**
26 (hardtop L)	$6,727	2,532	*
26 (hardtop GL)	$7,264	2,549	*
28 (hatchback GL)	$7,439	2,584	*
26 (notchback GLX)	$7,398	2,552	*
28 (hatchback GLX)	$7,557	2,587	*
27 (convertible GLX)	$9,449	2,759	*
28 (hatchback GT)	$9,328	2,891	*
27 (convertible GT)	$13,479	N/A	*
28 (hatchback Turbo GT)	$9,714	N/A	*
Year Total			120,873*

*Ford reports total production of 33,201 notchbacks, 64,234 hatchbacks and 23,438 convertibles.

1983 MUSTANG GLX CONVERTIBLE

1983 MUSTANG CONVERTIBLE

The biggest news of the year was the return of the convertible body style to the Mustang family. A midyear introduction available only in top-line GLX trim, it came complete with an electric top, a real glass rear window, and room for four. Advertising boasted, "It also comes complete with the wind in your hair and a pounding in your heart. And that makes it a Mustang." More than 20,000 sold in that abbreviated first year at a base price of $9,449 each.

Reluctant to commit wholesale to the untested topless car market, Ford subcontracted the ragtop conversion to Cars & Concepts of Brighton, Michigan. C&C received steel-topped notchbacks directly from the Ford factory. Convertibles could be ordered with any of the powertrains, except for the four-cylinder/automatic transmission combo.

Code	Engine	Intake	Power (hp)	Transmission
A	140-cid SOHC 4	1-bbl	90	M4, A3
T	140-cid SOHC 4 T	EFI	145	M4
3	232-cid V-6	2-bbl	105	M4, A3
F	302-cid V-8	4-bbl	175	M4

1983 Engines

1984 MUSTANG 20TH ANNIVERSARY "GT-350"

1984 MUSTANG

The GT came standard with increased power from the 5.0-liter H.O. V-8 (now rated at 175 hp in four-barrel form). A new, less-powerful version of the 302-cid V-8 joined the 1984 lineup.

Ford produced 5,260 20th Anniversary Mustangs around the GT package. Available only in Oxford White with Canyon Red interiors, the cars were further distinguished by articulated sports seats, rocker panel tape treatment that read "G.T. 350."

All Mustangs, starting in 1984, came equipped with Ford's new EEC-IV (electronic engine control system, fourth generation) that monitored engine functions.

1984 Production Chart

Model	Price	Weight	Production
26 (hardtop L)	$7,098	2,538	*
28 (hatchback L)	$7,269	2,584	*
26 (notchback LX)	$7,290	2,559	*
28 (hatchback LX)	$7,496	2,605	*
27 (convertible LX)	$11,849	2,873	*
28 (hatchback GT)	$9,762	2,753	*
27 (convertible GT)	$13,245	2,921	*
28 (hatchback SVO)	$15,596	2,881	4,508
Year Total			141,480*

*Ford reports total production of 37,680 notchbacks, 86,200 hatchbacks and 17,600 convertibles.

1984 Engines

Code	Engine	Intake	Power (hp)	Transmission
A	140-cid SOHC 4	1-bbl	88	M4, A3
T	140-cid SOHC 4 T	EFI	145	M4
W	140-cid SOHC 4 T SVO	EFI	175	M5
3	232-cid V-6	EFI	120	M4, A3
F	302-cid V-8	EFI	165	A3, A4
M	302-cid V-8	4-bbl	175	M5

1984 MUSTANG SVO

1984 SVO MUSTANG

Named for its creators in Ford's Special Vehicle Operations department, the SVO raised the bar on turbo technology with an air-to-air intercooler on its 2.3-liter turbocharged, fuel-injected four-cylinder engine. It was a package that produced 175 hp with improved low-end grunt. The SVO package included a Borg-Warner T-5 five-speed manual gearbox with Hurst linkage, four-wheel disc brakes, performance suspension with adjustable Koni gas-filled shocks, P225/50VR-16 Goodyear NCT tires on cast aluminum 16 x 7-inch wheels, and a functional hood scoop.

Test results showed the SVO could hit 134 miles per hour and get to 60 from a standstill in just 7.5 seconds. Inside were multi-adjustable articulated leather bucket seats. SVO's shock absorbers and struts had three settings: cross-country (for front and rear); GT (front only); and competition (front and rear). Four-wheel disc brakes were standard.

The SVO had a different front than the standard Mustang, with a grille-less fascia and integrated fog lamps. Just a single slot sat below the hood panel, which contained a Ford oval.

Large single rectangular headlamps were deeply recessed and flanked by large wraparound lenses. A polycarbonate, dual-wing rear spoiler was meant to increase downforce on the car at speed, while rear-wheel "spats" directed airflow around the wheel wells.

SVO's price tag was more than double that of a base Mustang four-cylinder. Offered in hatchback form only, SVO was available in Black, Silver Metallic, Dark Charcoal Metallic or Red Metallic. Interiors were all Charcoal. Only six major options were available for SVO: air conditioning; power windows; power door locks; cassette player; flip-up sunroof; and leather seat trim. Standard SVO equipment included an 8000-rpm tachometer; quick-ratio power steering and Traction-Lok rear axle. A premium/regular fuel switch calibrated the ignition instantly. Revised pedal positioning allowed "heel and toe" downshifting.

1984 SVO Production Chart			
Model	**Price**	**Weight**	**Production**
28 (hatchback SVO)	$15,596	2,881	4,508
Year Total			4,508

1984 MUSTANG SVO 2.3-LITER TURBO FOUR

1984 SVO MUSTANG ENGINE

SVO was formed in 1981 to supervise Ford's renewed involvement in motor sports (among other duties) and to develop special limited-edition high-performance vehicles. Its special turbo Mustang was the first of those offered as a production model. *Motor Trend* called the SVO "the best-driving street Mustang the factory has ever produced." Road & Track claimed the SVO "outruns the Datsun 280ZX, outhandles the Ferrari 308 and Porsche 944 ... and it's affordable." Its hefty price tag meant the SVO was targeted toward more affluent, car-conscious consumers.

Ad lines:
Built For Driving Enthusiasts By Driving Enthusiasts Straight from the Showroom, It's Far from "Stock."

1984 SVO Engine			
Code	**Engine**	**Power (hp)**	**Transmission**
W	140-cid (2.3-liter) EFI SOHC 4	175	M5

1984 SALEEN MUSTANG

1984 SALEEN MUSTANG

Steve Saleen, with a racing background in the Sports Car Club of America (SCCA) Formula Atlantic and Trans-Am series, was at the forefront of the American high-performance car movement in the mid-1980s. Saleen had owned '65 and '66 Shelby GT-350s and a '67 GT fastback with a 390-cid V-8, so he was quite aware of how Carroll Shelby had once turned a garden-variety Mustang into a world-class car.

Saleen elected to leave the engines stock and enhance performance by concentrating on suspension, brake, chassis, and aerodynamic improvements.

Saleen Autosport produced only three cars in 1984, each built from 175-hp Mustang hatchbacks. Saleen's own Racecraft suspension components, including specific-rate front and rear springs, Bilstein pressurized struts and shocks, a front G-load brace, and urethane sway bar bushings, lowered the car and improved the Mustang's handling to near racetrack levels. Those three '84s wore high-performance — Goodyear Eagle GTs measuring 215/60-15 wrapped around 15 x 7-inch Hayashi "basketweave" wheels. A custom front air dam, side skirts, and a showy spoiler created a smoother aerodynamic package. The interior featured a Saleen-unique gauge package, Wolf Racing four-spoke steering wheel and Escort radar detector.

The other standard equipment included a Saleen deck lid emblem, serial-numbered plaques, Ford Motorsport rear window graphic, tri-color racing stripes on the rocker panels, side window louvers, chrome air cleaner, 170-mph speedometer, Cal Custom Hawk leather-covered shift knob, Escort radar detector, and Cal Custom Hawk security system. The option was a Sanyo AM/FM stereo cassette player with speakers.

1984 Saleen Production Chart

Model	Price	Production
28 (hatchback)	$14,300	3
Year Total		3

1984 Saleen Engine

Code	Engine	Power (hp)	Transmission
M	302-cid (5.0-liter) V-8	175	M5

SALEEN ALUMINUM "BASKETWEAVE" WHEELS

SALEEN ALLOY WHEELS

Every Saleen Mustang, from the first 1984 to the latest supercharged S-281, has worn some form of cutting edge rim that generally outgrew Ford's standard wheel by an inch in diameter. In 1984, when the Mustang GT was still getting by with the five-year-old metric-sized TRX design or 14 x 5.5-inch 16-spoke aluminum models, Steve Saleen was installing 15 x 7-inch Hayashi rims. The lightweight design and larger diameter (complemented with "low-profile" 60-series Goodyear Eagle GTs) boosted the Mustang's so-so handling to an acceptably sporty level.

When Ford upgraded the GT to 15-inchers in 1985, Saleen offered optional 16-inch Enkeis with a basketweave, or "mesh," design, then switched to nearly identical Rikens in 1986. American Racing was the manufacturer of record for the 16-inchers Saleens wore from 1987

through 1991, before going through a couple of different 17-inch designs from Stern, Logic and Speedline through 1993. The only year Ford's and Saleen's versions of the Mustang wore the same size wheel during this period was in 1991, when the 5.0LX and GT came standard with a 16-inch five-spoke design.

Saleen leapt ahead of Ford's 17-inch GT wheels in 1994 with an 18-inch aluminum (magnesium optional) five-spoke on its S-351 super cars.

It is also noteworthy that all Saleen Mustang wheels are mounted with five lugs, except for years 1984 through 1986 when Ford's stock brake system was part of the Saleen package. Ford retained its disc/drum setup through model year 1993, but Saleen converted its cars to an all-disc system starting in 1987.

SALEEN RACECRAFT SUSPENSION

SALEEN RACECRAFT SUSPENSION

Named for Joe Carr's Racecraft fabrication shop in Petaluma, Calif., where the first Saleen Mustang was built, this special combination of springs, struts, shocks, bushings and alignment settings has taken many evolutionary steps since introduction.

In its first year the Racecraft formula utilized extremely stiff specific-rate front and rear coil springs (which lowered the car an inch), Bilstein pressurized struts and shocks and urethane sway bar pivot bushings front and rear. Some negative camber was dialed into the front alignment, which greatly improved the Mustang chassis' high-performance handling ability. Additionally, Saleen considers its upgraded wheels and tires to be part of the Racecraft package.

In 1989, Saleen added a cockpit-adjustable three-way (soft/medium/firm) feature to its Monroe-supplied Racecraft suspension components, although the upgrade was only available on that year's high-dollar SSC model; it would continue as an option across the board through 1993. Softer progressive-rate springs were introduced in the 1990 model year after customer feedback indicated the Saleen's harsh ride was the only drawback to ownership.

Racecraft parts dropped Saleen's S-351 a full three inches in 1994, but less radical springs were later introduced to appease customer complaints about the low ground clearance. Most S-351s and all S-281s were built with the 1.5-inch drop.

SALEEN BUMPER NUMBER

SALEEN SERIAL NUMBERS

Limited edition automobiles with any kind of enthusiast following are usually recognized by and discussed in terms of their individual serial numbers, the most studied example of which is the 1965 through 1970 Shelby Mustang. In order to keep his production line organized when it originally consisted of hundreds of solid white Mustang 2+2s, Carroll Shelby assigned each car a series-specific number such as SFM ("Shelby Ford Mustang") 5S071. This practice made the premium-priced, high-performance fastbacks seem just that much more special to their owners, but it also heightened the eventual collector market interest by creating a separate identity for each and every car.

In Shelby's case, each model year's run began with 001 and proceeded without intentional skips. When Steve Saleen built his first 1984 Mustang he wanted his one-man company to appear much larger and more successful than it really was, so he labeled vehicle 84-032 to suggest that 31 others had been built and sold. The other two Saleens built that year wore numbers 84-0051 and 84-0052.

Once his company began full production in 1985, the number system became standardized, although the first 10 digits each year were reserved for press vehicles, special customers and employee purchases. There never has been a Saleen number 0006, a tradition established due to an early typographical error.

Deciphering Saleen's numbering system requires some detective work, as unique production lines may or may not be considered separate by the company. For example, the 1989 SSC had its own set of numbers, but the supercharged 2000-and-later S/C is part of the standard line.

Every Saleen displays a number decal in front of the driver's-side headlight and on a plaque located on or near the console. Most have a plaque pop-riveted somewhere in the engine compartment, although early models were missing this identifying feature.

1985 MUSTANG GT CONVERTIBLE

1985 MUSTANG

Mustang performance only got hotter in 1985, with an unofficial theme of "More power!" throughout the lineup.

The GT's 5.0-liter H.O. V-8 benefited from a combination of old-fashioned hot rod tricks and new technology, enjoying a power boost to 210 hp through the use of low-friction roller tappets and a high-performance camshaft. Stainless steel headers replaced "high-flow" cast-iron manifolds, with twin pipes purging the hot exhaust gases through individual catalytic converters. What had been lost horsepower was regained through the use of a new accessory drive system that reduced the air-conditioner compressor, power steering pump, and alternator to half speed.

The fuel-injected version of the 5.0 (still only available with automatic transmission) produced 165 hp. 1985 marked the final year a four-barrel carburetor would appear on the 5.0-liter H.O. power plant before Ford followed the industry trend to fuel injection across the board. GT upgrades for 1985 included a

T-5 transmission with shorter gear throws, a quad-shock system in the rear, a larger rear stabilizer bar, and Goodyear Eagle P225/60VR-15 "Gatorback" unidirectional tires mounted on new alloy wheels.

All 1985 Mustangs wore a new front-end look with a four-hole integral air dam below the bumper, flanked by low rectangular parking lamps. GTs also sported integral fog lamps. A grille similar to the one on the SVO–essentially one wide slot with angled sides in a sloping front panel–appeared on all Mustangs displaying a Ford oval. Tail lamps were full-width (except for the license plate opening), with backup lenses at the upper portion of each inner section. A Ford script oval stood above the right tail lamp. Most Mustang exterior trim and accents switched from black to a softer charcoal shade. All models had new charcoal front and rear bumper rub strips and body side moldings. Also new were a charcoal hood paint/tape treatment, a revised deck lid decal, and GT nomenclature (where applicable) molded into the body side strip.

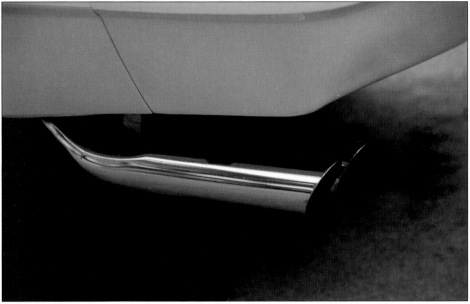

1985 MUSTANG DUAL EXHAUST

DUAL EXHAUST SYSTEM

Ford knows its enthusiastic Mustang buyers associate a dual exhaust system with performance, which is why its designers and engineers installed some form of twin pipes on every sporty Fox V-8 model built since 1979.

For the first six years, the "Fox"-body Mustangs with V-8 power merely had the appearance of a dual exhaust system as that's how many shiny metal outlets protruded from the rear of the car. In reality, the 5.0-liter (and lowly 4.2-liter from 1980 and '81) engines fed their hot exhaust gases through a cast iron manifold into individual pipes that immediately dumped into a single conduit. From there a solitary tube connected to a catalytic converter and ultimately to a lone muffler outfitted with two tailpipes. It was hardly the high-flow system enthusiasts

had been dreaming about since the early 1970s, but Ford advertising tiptoed around the subject, always suggesting but never verifying.

Part of the Mustang's 35-hpincrease in 1985 was due to a "nearly true" dual exhaust setup that ran stainless steel headers in front of a single converter that split into twin pipes and mufflers. Beefy tailpipes pointed straight out the rear of the car just below bumper level like a pair of bazookas locking in on a target.

In 1986 Ford switched the Mustang to a true dual system, with a manifold, converter, muffler and tailpipe for each engine bank. Borrowing from its '60s muscle car days, Ford installed an H-pipe near the converter to balance the flow of gases from one tube to the other.

1985 MUSTANG TWISTER II

SPECIAL EDITIONS

Mustang performance revitalized Ford's image in the mid-1980s. The 1985 model was particularly popular with enthusiasts; Ford had forecast the sale of 128,000 units that year, but 156,514 went to new homes. Mustang production accounted for an impressive 2 percent of industry output for 1985, 31.7 percent of which were powered by the more expensive V-8s. Other engine installations broke down to 55.5 percent four-cylinders and 12.7 percent V-6s.

One ingredient in Ford's recipe for success was the range of cosmetic and performance packages available. Far from being just a single model in the corporate line, the Mustang had become its own brand and could be ordered as plain, pumped or pimped as the customer desired.

Ford produced a limited run of 90 Twister II GTs by request of the Kansas City regional dealers to commemorate the 15th anniversary of the original Twister promotional Mustang. All Twister IIs were built on 5.0 GT chassis, the majority of which (74) were hatchbacks with five-speed manuals, followed by convertibles with five-speeds (9), convertible automatics (5) and convertible five-speeds (2). There were absolutely no mechanical differences between a standard GT and a Twister II. The special model received unique tornado-like graphics, a dash plaque, a commemorative coaster and a Ford press kit.

Colors were limited to Jalapeno Red, Medium Canyon Red Metallic, Oxford White and Silver Metallic.

1985 LX 5.0-LITER CONVERTIBLE

1985 LX 5.0

For 1985, the base L series was dropped, making LX the bottom-level Mustang and GT the performance model.

Standard LX equipment now included power brakes and steering; dual-note horn; interval windshield wipers; and an AM/FM stereo radio. As before notchback, hatchback and convertible bodies were offered. New standard interior features included a console; low-back bucket seats (on LX); luxury door trim panels; and covered visor mirrors.

Ordering an LX with the 5.0-liter V-8 included all of the GT's mechanical components such as 15-inch Goodyear Eagle 225/60VR15 Gatorback tires and new 10-spoke alloy wheels — around $1,400 cheaper than the GT. Because the cheaper model came equipped with fewer standard features than the GT it was argued that the lighter base LX with 5.0-liter V-8 was a faster car.

1985 Production Chart

Model	Price	Weight	Production
26 (notchback LX)	$6,885	2,559	*
28 (hatchback LX)	$7,345	2,605	*
27 (convertible LX)	$11,985	2,873	*
28 (hatchback GT)	$9,885	2,899	*
27 (convertible GT)	$13,585	3,043	*
28 (hatchback SVO)	$14,521	2,881	1,954
Year Total			156,514*

*Ford reports total production of 56,781 notchbacks, 84,623 hatchbacks and 15,110 convertibles.

1985 Engines

Code	Engine	Intake	Power (hp)	Transmission
A	140-cid SOHC 4	1-bbl	88	M5, A3
W	140-cid SOHC 4 T SVO	EFI	205	M5
3	232-cid V-6	EFI	120	M4, A4
M	302-cid V-8	EFI	165	A4
M	302-cid V-8	4-bbl	210	M5

MUSTANG 15-INCH ALUMINUM WHEEL

10-HOLE WHEEL

The odd-size TRX wheel package was re-tired at the end of 1984, and in its place at the top of the Mustang's high-performance equipment list Ford introduced a 15 x 7-inch cast-aluminum rim. All 1985 GTs received this "10-hole" design right away, but it was not until mid year that it became a mandatory part of the 5.0 LX package.

V-8 Mustangs benefited from improved tire technology in the form of wide P225/60VR15 Goodyear Eagle "Gatorback" tires (first seen on the 1984 SVO) wrapped around the new wheel.

The popular 15-inch wheel was the 5.0 LX and GT standard rim from 1985 through 86. In 1987, the GT received its own unique wheel, but the LX V-8 cars continued to be fitted with the 10-hole through 1990. From 1991 through 1992 it was an optional wheel for any four-cylinder model.

1985½ SVO MUSTANG

1985½ SVO MUSTANG

SVO engineers treated their self-named Mustang model midyear to a new look (primarily flush-mounted headlamps) and an impressive 205 hp. Once again, hot rod met high-tech under the hood with a higher-performance cam, higher-flow exhaust system, reconfigured turbocharger, larger injectors, and greater boost accounting for the increase.

Race driver Jackie Stewart, a Ford consultant, promoted "The New Turbo Math" in an advertisement for the SVO. He said "Proven in race cars, the intercooled turbo is now in the Mustang SVO, the only American production car to have this kind of turbo. Ford is in the forefront of this new turbo technology." The price of the all-out sports car dropped slightly, to $14,521, but sales also fell to 1,954 units.

Ad lines:
Competition-Tested Components Remove All Doubt Mustang SVO is Automotive Sophistication at its Best

1985½ SVO Production Chart

Model	Price	Weight	Production
28 (hatchback SVO)	$14,521	2,881	1,954
Year Total			1,954

1985½ SVO Engine

Code	Engine	Power (hp)	Transmission
W	140-cid (2.3-liter) EFI SOHC 4	205	M5

1985 SALEEN MUSTANG

1985 SALEEN

The 1985 Saleen, which was based on Ford's new 210-horsepower 5.0-liter LX and GT, featured larger 225/60-15 Goodyear or Fulda tires (depending on time of production) and a slightly modified aerodynamics package. Sales for the $16,900 Saleen were improved with 140 units going to new owners, including two convertibles.

Available standard Saleen colors included Ford's Black, Canyon Red, Medium Regatta Blue, or Oxford White. Special-ordered paint cost an additional $150, and building the car on a Mustang GT was an additional $100.

Saleen arranged a bailment pooling agreement with Ford in 1985, meaning cars could be sold through the company's established dealer network with full warranty protection.

Participating dealers were advised to order cars intended for Saleen conversion with the M-code 5.0-liter V-8, 3.08:1 limited-slip axle, five-speed transmission, and 225/60VR-15 Goodyear Gatorbacks.

Running production year changes were common with early Saleens. Cars converted early in the year were modified in a shop in Petaluma, California, north of the San Francisco area, while the remaining 1985 production took place at the Burch Ford dealership in LaHabra, in southern California.

1985 Saleen Production Chart

Model	Price	Production
28 (hatchback)	$16,900	138*
27 (convertible)	$18,900	2
Year Total		140*

*Figures reflect five cars listed with the company as "unknown." Output includes 1 competition model.

1985 Saleen Engines

Code	Engine	Power (hp)	Transmission
M	302-cid (5.0-liter) V-8	210	M5
M	302-cid (5.0-liter) V-8	165	A4

1986 MUSTANG GT

1986 MUSTANG

The Mustang's appearance was essentially the same as in the previous year. The sloping center front-end panel held a Ford oval at the top, and a wide single opening below. The quad rectangular headlamps were deeply recessed. Parking lamps stood far down on the front end. Side marker lenses were angled to match the front fender tips. Tail lamps were distinctly split into upper and lower sections by a full-width divider bar. "Mustang" lettering sat above the left tail lamp and a Ford oval above the right.

The GT included a special suspension, Goodyear Eagle VR performance tires, quick-ratio power steering, and articulated front sport seats. For 1986, the wide grey GT hood stripe could be deleted on request of the customer. The LX came standard with full body side striping, power brakes and steering, and extras such as interval wipers, luxury sound package, and an AM/FM stereo radio (which could be deleted for credit).

Turbine wheel covers switched from bright/argent to bright/black. The Mustang's rear axle

was upgraded to 8.8 inches with the standard 2.73:1 axle ratio or optional 3.08:1 (cars with automatic transmissions were equipped with 3.27:1 rear gears), for use with the 5.0-liter V-8. Viscous engine mounts were added on the 3.8-liter V-6 and the V-8, as had been used on the turbo four starting in mid-year 1985. Ford boosted its anti-corrosion warranty, added sound-deadening material, and adopted a single-key lock system.

1986 Production Chart

Model	Price	Weight	Production
26 (notchback LX)	$7,189	2,601	*
28 (hatchback LX)	$7,744	2,661	*
27 (convertible LX)	$12,821	2,908	*
28 (hatchback GT)	$10,691	2,976	*
27 (convertible GT)	$14,523	3,103	*
28 (hatchback SVO)	$15,272	3,028	3,382
Year Total			244,410

*Ford reports total production of 84,774 notchbacks, 22,946 convertibles and 117,690 hatchbacks.

1986 MUSTANG LX 5.0 HARDTOP

MUSTANG COUPES

Much has been made of the GT's 1982 revival and subsequent dominance of the American muscle car scene, but little attention has been paid to the Mustang that enjoyed a better power-to-weight ratio and acceleration times than the top-line pony.

Each year between 1982 and the end of "Fox-body production in 1993, any customer could order the GT's 5.0-liter V-8, five-speed transmission, optional performance rear axle gears and suspension/tires on a notchback sedan (the LX, as of 1985 and later) for a savings of several hundred pounds and a substantial amount of cash. Coupes also had stiffer chassis than the hatchbacks or convertibles, which made them great handlers.

Due to low demand, Ford never produced many Mustangs in coupe form compared to the hatchback. For example, 84,623 three-door models were built in 1985, but only 56,781 notchbacks. The difference was even more dramatic by 1993, when Ford sold 62,077 hatchbacks and 24,851 coupes.

The LX hatchback offered greater versatility for travel and packing, which no doubt convinced many buyers to overlook the LX coupe's more athletic abilities. The 1987-and-later GT had look-at-me graphics and ground effects to draw attention away from its plainer sister.

Today, young Mustang fans look for the V-8 coupes because of their unique styling and performance edge.

1986 MUSTANG 5.0-LITER V-8

5.0-LITER EFI V-8

Gone was the four-barrel 5.0-liter H.O. for 1986, and taking its place was the sequential port fuel injected 5.0-liter H.O. rated at 200 hp and 285 lbs.-ft. of torque. In addition to the new induction system, the H.O. benefited from re-designed heads, an improved water pump and a stronger block design. The new V-8 was standard in the GT and an extra-cost option for the LX. All Mustang V-8 models with five-speed manual transmissions also received an indicator light to tell drivers when to shift gears for maximum fuel economy.

The GT came in for some criticism in 1986 for losing 10 hp on paper, but the 15 lbs.-ft. increase in torque output and smoother power delivery made it an easier car to drive slowly or quickly. A new head design was necessary for the 5.0-liter to meet certain emissions and fuel efficiency requirements, which explains the horsepower drop. This low-flow head was replaced in '87.

The new V-8 could be hooked to a five-speed manual (overdrive) Borg-Warner T-5 transmission or four-speed automatic overdrive.

The throttle-body-injected V-6 with 120 hp was standard in LX ragtops and optional in other models. Base engine remained the 2.3-liter four, which was mated to a five-speed manual transmission or optional three-speed automatic.

1986 Engines				
Code	Engine	Intake	Power (hp)	Transmission
A	140-cid SOHC 4	1-bbl	88	M5, A3
W	140-cid SOHC 4 T SVO	EFI	205	M5
3	232-cid V-6	EFI	120	M4, A4
M	302-cid V-8	EFI	200	M5, A4

1986 SVO MUSTANG

1986 SVO MUSTANG

During its final year of production, 1986, the SVO received more conservative programming of its EEC-IV, which dropped the horsepower rating to 200@5,000 rpm. The SVO Mustang's appearance was essentially the same as the year before. Ford boosted its anti-corrosion warranty, added sound-deadening material and

Ad lines:

The Machine Speaks for Itself
Sophistication, Performance, Value

adopted a single-key lock system. A third, high-mounted brake lamp was a new safety feature made mandatory for 1986, and the SVO integrated the light into its rear spoiler.

Ford sold 3,382 1986 SVOs with a base price of $15,272, for a three-year total of 9,844 cars.

1986 SVO Production Chart

Model	Price	Weight	Production
28 (hatchback SVO)	$15,272	3,028	3,382
Year Total			3,382

1986 SVO Engine

Code	Engine	Power (hp)	Transmission
W	140-cid (2.3-liter) EFI SOHC 4	205	M5

1986 SPECIAL SERVICE VEHICLE MUSTANG

SPECIAL SERVICE VEHICLE MUSTANG

No Mustang is surrounded by as much mystery and misinformation as the Special Service Vehicle (SSV) program cars. People still like to tell stories about being pulled over by state troopers in "hopped up" 5.0-liter Mustangs that had blueprinted engines, special cams, race-ready brakes and other intriguing equipment.

There's a problem with these memories — they just aren't true!

In 1982, Ford won a bid against Chevrolet's Camaro to supply the California Highway Patrol with Mustangs for high-speed pursuit, all of which were mechanically stock. The cost of modifying an assembly line engine, paying for emissions certification and keeping enough spare parts on hand for maintenance — all to sell a few thousand extra cars around the country each year–was prohibitive and unnecessary. As the years progressed, certain heavy-duty items such as hoses and belts and thicker floor pans were installed on these SSVs, which were also known generically as police interceptors and pursuit vehicles. There were no changes made to the powertrain with the goal of generating more power or speed.

California's 1982 cars were L-series notchbacks with the 157-hp 5.0-liter purchased for $6,868 each. With the purchase of these Mustang coupes, the CHP was finally able to catch speeders driving the sporty imports that are so common on California's freeways. The rest of the country was impressed enough to follow the West Coast's example. From 1982 to 1993, Ford produced more than 15,000 SSVs for nearly three-dozen states.

The Mustangs were universally praised for their performance, reliability and handling and many police officers and state troopers expressed regret at giving them up.

1986 MUSTANG 5.0-LITER V-8 AIRBOX

THE 5.0 AIRBOX

For the new electronically managed EFI 5.0-liter to run efficiently, it was necessary to supply it with a consistent volume and temperature of oxygen from the atmosphere, which meant locating the air pickup point as far from the heat of the engine as possible.

Engineers moved the 1986 Mustang V-8's battery from its traditional place just behind the passenger-side headlamp and installed there a plastic rectangular air filter housing. Clamped to the airbox, but hidden from view within the fender well was a plastic baffle, or "air horn," whose purpose was to slow and straighten the

gas flow before it hit the filter. The baffle was responsible for reducing under hood noise from the induction process, but it also killed 5 to 7 hp and was often removed by the Mustang's owner shortly after purchase.

Many "Mustangers" also took the inexpensive step of replacing the stock Ford paper air filter with a high-flow, reusable fabric unit. (K&N was a popular choice).

The black rectangular airbox was standard under hood issue from introduction in 1986 to the end of '93.

CENTER HIGH-MOUNTED STOP LIGHT (CHMSL)

CHMSL (CENTER HIGH-MOUNTED STOP LIGHTS)

All cars sold in America in 1986 were fitted with center high-mounted stop lights (CHMSL). Some manufacturers, such as Mazda with its RX-7, had new designs being introduced that year and were able to incorporate the mandatory safety feature into their cars' bodies without drawing attention to them.

Others, such as Ford with its "Fox"-based Mustang, were in the middle of a long production cycle and had to attach the conspicuous red signals with little regard for aesthetics. The company installed CHMSLs on the inside package trays of LX coupes; in the spoilers of GTs and LX hatchbacks; and on the now-mandatory luggage racks of GT and LX convertibles.

1986 SALEEN MUSTANG

1986 SALEEN

Ford converted its Mustang V-8 to electronic fuel injection for 1986, a change reflected in the cars Steve Saleen was building in California. Competition in Sports Car Club of America (SCCA) races brought about high-performance improvements such as 16-inch wheels, a revised air dam and spoiler package, GT bucket seats, and Koni adjustable gas rear shocks. A race-style "dead pedal" for the driver's left foot became standard Saleen equipment in 1986.

Well-equipped, Saleens had few options: a Kenwood KRC 6000 AM/FM cassette stereo system, an automatic transmission, sunroof and certain aftermarket performance enhancements. Many cars were built without the Hurst shifter (due to a vendor shortage).

Exterior colors available were Black, Canyon Red, Medium Regatta Blue, and Oxford White. On red and white cars the side louvers behind the rear window were painted body color. The tri-color racing stripes were available in gold, silver or blue. Ford dealers ordered cars for conversion as LX hatchback or convertible, 5.0-liter V-8, five-speed manual transmission, 3.08:1 limited-slip axle, 225/60VR-15 tires, radio delete, articulated sport seats, GT dash panel, SVO driver's foot rest and pinstripe delete.

Despite a 10-horsepower deficit below the 1985 model, magazine testers were impressed with the package's 6.0-second 0-to-60 mph time and top speed of 142 mph. Sales continued to increase, with 190 coupes and 11 convertibles going to new customers.

1986 Saleen Engine			
Code	Engine	Power (hp)	Transmission
M	302-cid (5.0-liter) V-8	200	M5, A4

1986 Saleen Production Chart		
Model	Price	Production
28 (hatchback)	$17,900	190*
27 (convertible)	$19,900	11
Year Total		201
*Output includes 3 competition models.		

1987 MUSTANG GT CONVERTIBLE

1987 MUSTANG

It is truly frightening to realize that the 1987 Mustang came very close to being the last of a breed. Earlier in the 1980s, Ford corporate planners developed a project named "SN8" (Ford-speak for sporty, North American project no. 8) to replace the Mustang's rear-drive "Fox" platform with a small, high-tech, European-style chassis. This scheme was not approved but another plan was soon hatched to have Japanese partner Mazda develop a similar platform that would be shared between the two companies and built in a plant in Flat Rock, Michigan.

Ford was concerned about getting caught in the middle of another fuel crisis with showrooms full of thirsty V-8 performance cars. Otherwise, it would not have spent so many development and marketing dollars on the 1979 through 1986 turbocharged models. Chrysler earned its financial salvation by selling millions of bog-slow four-cylinder K-cars in the early 1980s. Ford went from red ink to billions of dollars in cash reserves by creating an exciting, balanced, product line anchored by its top-selling Taurus.

Plans for a "next-generation" Mustang could be executed for many millions of dollars less if Mazda's innovative engineering and production were utilized. Mazda stood to benefit from the deal by further aligning itself with an American corporate giant and perhaps escape the brunt of threatened import taxes and tariffs.

The public, informed through several well-placed magazine articles, quickly clued Ford in on how it felt about keeping the Mustang alive, rear-wheel drive and all-American. Ford quickly changed tack and gave the front-drive Japanese-engineered car a "Probe" nameplate on its introduction as a 1989 model. Ford never reported losing Mustang sales to the Probe or vice versa. Apparently, there weren't a lot of customers who saw the choices as similar. Mazda's version of the shared platform was the MX-6.

1987-'93 MUSTANG 225-HORSEPOWER 5.0-LITER V-8

225-HORSEPOWER 5.0-LITER V-8

The standard engine in the base LX model notchbacks, hatchbacks and convertibles was the sturdy 2.3-liter four, improved for 1987 with a new multi-port fuel-injection system. Its output was up slightly to 90 hp and 130 lbs.-ft. of torque.

Optional in LX models and standard in GTs was a 225-hp 5.0-liter V-8. Ford engineers replaced the 1986 5.0-liter heads with an earlier, better flowing design and gained 25 horsepower.

There would be almost no change to the Mustang's V-8 for the next seven years.

The V-6 and turbocharged four from 1986 were no longer offered. The SVO was gone, but the LX coupe with the 5.0-liter H.O. V-8 seemed nearly as exciting to speed freaks on a budget.

Also gone were the myriad choices of power plant and model combinations. Both 1987 Mustang engines came with either a five-speed manual or an optional automatic overdrive transmission.

1987 Production Chart			
Model	**Price**	**Weight**	**Production**
40 (notchback LX)	$8,043	2,724	*
41 (hatchback LX)	$8,474	2,782	*
44 (convertible LX)	$12,840	2,921	*
42 (hatchback GT)	$11,835	3,080	*
45 (convertible GT)	$15,724	3,214	*
Year Total			244,410*
*Ford reports total production of 43,275 notchbacks, 32,074 convertibles and 94,441 hatchbacks.			

1987 Engines				
Code	**Engine**	**Intake**	**Power (hp)**	**Transmission**
A	140-cid SOHC 4	EFI	90	M5, A3
M	302-cid V-8	EFI	225	M5, A4

1987-'93 MUSTANG GT LOUVERED TAILLIGHTS

STYLING CHANGES

Ford's "Fox"-bodied pony car received a fresh look for 1987 with the first significant restyling since its debut in 1979. No one outside of Ford Motor Company could predict at the time that the new look would endure with very little change for the next seven years!

The attractive 1987 revamp included new front and rear body fascias, aero headlamps and a prominent lower feature line accented with heavy moldings. The wind tunnel loved the car, with a base hatchback registering a 0.36 drag coefficient (compared to the 1979 model's 0.44) and the bulky GT three-door turning out a 0.38.

Other changes inside the Mustang were a redesigned instrument panel that created a roomier passenger compartment, pod-mounted headlamp switches, and a center console.

The new Mustang retained a 100.5-inch wheelbase and 179-inch overall length. It was 68.3 inches wide and about 52 inches high (depending on body style) with a track of 56.6 inches in the front and 57 inches in the rear. Weights for various models ranged from 2,724 pounds (base coupe) to 3,214 lbs. (GT convertible), roughly a 100-pound increase model-to-model over 1986 specs.

1987-'90 MUSTANG GT 16-SPOKE/16-INCH WHEEL

16-SPOKE GT WHEEL

A big part of Ford's program to set the 1987 GT apart from the cheaper LX was the creation of a unique aerodynamic and cosmetic package. The choice of a new wheel also played a major role in distinguishing the GT as a top-drawer model, and it was one of the first attempts Ford made at bringing a "retro" look to the Mustang.

Although it looked larger than the old GT 10-spoke rim, the new 16-vane design retained the 15 x 7-inch dimensions and wore the same P225/60VR15 Goodyear Eagle Gatorback high-performance radials. The busy spoke pattern of the new design perfectly matched the GT's louvered taillight treatment and deeply ridged front spoiler, but made it a real pain to keep clean.

The 16-vane design belonged entirely to the GT until 1990's run of limited edition Deep Emerald Jewel Green convertibles was fitted with them. In 1991, when the GT and LX 5.0 received the 16-inch, five-spoke wheel, Ford dropped the 16-vane design entirely.

1987 SALEEN MUSTANG

1987 SALEEN

Saleen Mustangs benefited from improvements to the platform in 1987, with changes that included a 225-hp V-8 engine and a slightly more aerodynamic body. The addition of four-wheel disc brakes and stronger five-lug rotors made that year's limited edition offering so enticing to performance enthusiasts.

Beautiful alloy American Racing "basket weave" wheels, measuring 16 x 7 inches (front) and 16 x 8 inches (rear), were wrapped by 225/50VR-16 General XP-2000 high-performance tires. Saleen's Racecraft suspension system included specific-rate front and rear coil springs, Koni shocks all around, special strut mounting bearings, urethane sway bar pivot bushing and high-performance alignment specs.

The chassis was also tightened.

Without modifying the 5.0-liter engine, Saleen Mustangs generated quicker acceleration times than stock ponies due to chassis stiffeners, stronger suspension and the new-for-1987 option of 3.55:1 rear axle gears.

Saleen interior upgrades included installation of articulated FloFit seats, and a three-spoke Momo steering wheel. The Escort radar detector came off the standard equipment list and became an option.

Sales of the Saleen were brisk at 280 copies.

1987 Saleen Engine			
Code	Engine	Power (hp)	Transmission
M	302-cid (5.0-liter) V-8	225	M5, A4

1987 Saleen Production Chart		
Model	Price	Production
41 (hatchback)	$20,999	246*
44 (convertible)	$22,999	33
40 (coupe)	N/A	1
Year Total		280
*Output includes 6 competition models.		

1987-'93 SALEEN MUSTANG DISC BRAKES

SALEEN FOUR-WHEEL DISC BRAKES

In 1987 the Fox-generation Mustang was equipped with its most powerful engine ever, but Ford still neglected to address the obvious shortcomings of the eight-year-old chassis: its rear drum brakes and four-lug rotors.

As an SCCA Showroom Stock Mustang racer, Steve Saleen had a very strong opinion about the factory's brake system — he hated it! Not only did the small front disc and rear drum overheat on the race track, but during a race at Nelson Ledges Saleen's car lost a wheel when the weak four-lug system let loose.

Wanting to take his 1987 high-performance Mustang package to a new level, Saleen developed a brake system using Lincoln, Thunderbird and SVO components that produced a shorter stopping distance (by five feet from 60 miles per hour) and were virtually fade resistant. The fact that those parts incorporated a stronger five-lug arrangement was a bonus enthusiastic drivers could appreciate.

So involved was the changeover in parts that only the original brake pedal itself remained after conversion to Saleen specs. As was established company protocol, the four-wheel disc system was tested on Steve Saleen's personal car — an '85 hatchback that received the brake upgrade late in 1986. It was tested on and off the track before going into production.

Bolted to the new rotors was a set of American Racing basketweave wheels measuring 16 x 7 inches in the front and 16 x 8 inches in the rear with General XP2000 P225/50VR16 high-performance radials all around.

With the move to an all-disc system, Saleen Autosport became SVO's biggest customer in 1987.

1987-'91 SALEEN MUSTANG FLOFIT SEATS

SALEEN FLOFIT SEATS

From 1984 through the end of model year 1986, Saleen Mustangs were available with a variety of bucket seats, all based on stock Ford components. Most were equipped with cloth seats from the base or GT Mustangs, but some customers paid extra for leather. There was even a retro "lowback" option from which the rectangular head restraints were removed.

In 1987 Steve Saleen began a long relationship with Long Beach Motoring Accessories, the United States importer of FloFit seats. The articulated buckets had a sportier feel than anything Ford was installing at the time, and they sat firmer. Eager to create a complete performance image for his cars, Saleen developed a unique fabric through FloFit that was also used to cover the Mustang's stock back seat cushions.

With this final ingredient in the recipe, everything the driver touched—the seat, stick shift and steering wheel –were designed and installed by Saleen Autosport. Leather FloFits were standard equipment on the 1989 SSC, but continued as an extra-cost option on the regular Saleens.

Because German manufacturer Recaro had such name recognition as a maker of sport seats, many enthusiasts have incorrectly referred to the Saleen chairs as such, but FloFit was the supplier of record from 1987 through 1991.

1988 MUSTANG LX 5.0 HATCHBACK

1988 MUSTANG

1988 was the second of many years Ford would bring the Mustang to market virtually unchanged from its 1987 restyling. With such a successful package, who could blame them?

The same three body styles were again offered in LX trim, with a pair of GTs (not offered in coupe form) also available. Prices jumped around $700 per closed model and around $1,100 for ragtops. The cars ranged from $8,726 up to $16,610. This was a boom year for the Mustang, as model year output zoomed to 211,225 cars.

The same two engine choices remained: the basic 2.3-liter four-cylinder or the pavement-pounding 5.0-liter H.O. V-8.

1988 Production Chart			
Model	**Price**	**Weight**	**Production**
40 (notchback LX)	$8,726	2,751	*
41 (hatchback LX)	$9,221	2,818	*
44 (convertible LX)	$13,702	2,953	*
42 (hatchback GT)	$12,745	3,193	*
45 (convertible GT)	$16,610	3,341	*
Year Total			211,225*

*Ford reports total production of 53,221 notchbacks, 32,074 convertibles and 125,930 hatchbacks.

1988 Engines				
Code	**Engine**	**Intake**	**Power (hp)**	**Transmission**
A	140-cid SOHC 4	EFI	90	M5, A3
M	302-cid V-8	EFI	225	M5, A4

1988 MUSTANG LX CONVERTIBLE

1988 LX CONVERTIBLE

Ford advertisements for its 1988 Mustang LX convertible sounded like the company was attempting to hypnotize customers into the showroom.

"You're driving down the road under a cool evening sky. The wind in your hair, the moon on your face, and the stars in your eyes. The music is up as you sit back in a comfortable bucket seat, surrounded by a finely detailed interior. The feeling is out of this world. And off you go."

Another ad featuring a base LX convertible reads like a visit to the dentist's office:

"It's just what the doctor ordered... plenty of fresh air, fun and relaxation. The Ford Mustang LX Convertible. Power window, power door locks, power mirrors... the easy life... The Ford LX Mustang Convertible. 'Ahhh...'"

1988 SALEEN MUSTANG HARDTOP

1988 SALEEN HARDTOP

The 1988 Saleens were essentially carryovers from the previous year. Steve Saleen replaced the Koni shocks with Monroe units on his street cars after Monroes helped his racecars turn faster lap times and American-built Pioneer got the nod to replace Kenwood as the official stereo supplier.

The Racecraft suspension system included the '87 specific-rate front and rear coil springs, Monroe shocks all around, special strut mounting bearings, urethane sway bar pivot bushing and high-performance alignment specs. Other standard equipment included 225/50VR-16 General XP-2000V tires, Monroe quad shocks, Saleen aerodynamic kit, 170-mph speedometer, Hurst quick-ratio shifter, articulated FloFit sport seats, three-spoke Momo steering wheel and a Saleen Mustang jacket. The standard stereo was a Pioneer KEH 6050 AM/FM system with cassette player, Pioneer BP 880 graphic equalizer and six speakers.

The only option listed by the factory was the 3.55:1 rear axle, although customers could make special requests such as automatic transmissions, sunroofs and certain aftermarket performance enhancements. Running changes through the production year were minimal.

It was no surprise that 708 Saleens were sold in '88, including 137 convertibles and 25 coupes.

1988 Saleen Production Chart		
Model	**Price**	**Production**
41 (hatchback)	$21,500	546*
44 (convertible)	$24,950	137
40 (coupe)	N/A	25
Year Total		708

*Output includes 3 competition models.

1988 Saleen Engine			
Code	**Engine**	**Power (hp)**	**Transmission**
M	302-cid (5.0-liter) V-8	225	M5, A4

1988-'91 SALEEN MUSTANG 16-INCH WHEEL

SALEEN 16-INCH FIVE-SPOKE WHEEL

Choices were slim in the automotive high-performance world of the mid-1980s. It was a time when very little was available off the shelf for American cars, particularly the popular Mustang. In those days the easiest way to create a strong but lightweight wheel was through an interlocking mesh or "basketweave" design. Its thin aluminum planes acted to reinforce each other just like the metal spokes on earlier wire knockoffs.

German manufacturer BBS was a pioneer in alloy wheel production most closely associated with the mesh design, an elegant piece that found its way onto modified BMWs and Ferraris. When a Hayashi-built version of the rim appeared on the first Saleen Mustang, it gave the high-performance pony a European flair while reducing unsprung weight on the corners and allowing for a lower profile tire.

The next evolutionary step in lightweight wheels for performance applications came when Ronal introduced a clean five-spoke "star" design. Saleen Autosport announced that such a wheel would be available with its 1987 model line (and even featured it in some advertising), but the American Racing-built five-spokes would not appear on customer cars until the end of 1988 production.

That basic five-spoke became the only standard wheel in 1990, then was dropped at the end of the 1991 model year. The 1989 SSC and 1990 and '91 SC wore a different, softer five-spoke design produced by DP.

1989 MUSTANG GT HATCHBACK

1989 MUSTANG

1989 will always be remembered by Mustang enthusiasts as the year Ford "forgot" the car's 25th birthday. When the Mustang went into its silver anniversary year, the parent company did not issue a commemorative model, although magazines, fans, and performance authorities as revered as Jack Roush and Steve Saleen suggested that it do so.

Appearing late in the model year were 3,600 1990 5.0-liter LX convertibles decked out in Emerald Green with white interiors and tiny badges indicating the 25th anniversary.

The base Mustang LX was fun to drive with its responsive 2.3-liter four-cylinder engine, a five-speed manual transmission, power front disc brakes, modified MacPherson strut suspension, 20.0:1-ratio rack-and-pinion power steering, styled road wheels, and P195/75R-14 black sidewall steel-belted radial tires. Comfortable interiors with cloth reclining seats were standard.

The three-model line had list prices from $9,050 to $17,512, and with the optional Special Value Group buyers got power locks, dual electric mirrors, an electronic AM/FM stereo with a cassette tape player, and more.

1989 Production Chart

Model	Price	Weight	Production
40 (notchback LX)	$9,050	2,754	*
41 (hatchback LX)	$9,556	2,819	*
44 (convertible LX)	$14,140	2,966	*
42 (hatchback GT)	$13,272	3,194	*
45 (convertible GT)	$17,512	3,333	*
Year Total			209,769*

*Ford reports total production of 50,560 notchbacks, 42,244 convertibles and 116,965 hatchbacks.

1989 Engines

Code	Engine	Intake	Power (hp)	Transmission
A	140-cid SOHC 4	EFI	90	M5, A3
M	302-cid V-8	EFI	225	M5, A4

1989 SALEEN MUSTANG

1989 SALEEN MUSTANG

Saleen Autosport was a company on fire in 1989, its growth outlook for the year including record sales of the popular Mustang conversion, another attempt at an SCCA championship, an Indy Car campaign, and the introduction of the highly anticipated Saleen SSC super car.

1989 Saleen Mustangs were essentially carryovers from 1988 with minimal changes. The Racecraft suspension system included specific-rate front and rear coil springs, Monroe shocks all around, special strut mounting bearings, urethane sway bar pivot bushing, and high-performance alignment specs. The standard stereo was a Pioneer KEH 6050 AM/FM system with cassette player, Pioneer BP 880 graphic equalizer, and six speakers. Other standard equipment included 225/50VR-16 General XP-2000V tires, Monroe quad shocks, Saleen aerodynamic kit, 170-mph speedometer, Hurst quick-ratio shifter, articulated FloFit sport seats, and a three-spoke Momo steering wheel (in its final year).

The only options listed by the factory were the 3.27:1 limited-slip differential, the 3.55:1 limited-slip axle, a heavy-duty radiator and cooling system and a Panhard rod. Customers could request an automatic transmission, a sunroof, and other aftermarket performance enhancements. Special five-spoke, 16-inch wheels became available early in the year. For the first time, Saleen buyers had the option of cruise control.

Sales for the standard conversion added up to 734 cars, including four specially-built hatchbacks for Pioneer (although standard Saleens, they resembled SSCs), two ordered by Eagle 1 for giveaways and one ordered by General Tire. On the track, the SCCA campaign was still successful and continuing to build the high-performance image of the base Saleen Mustang.

1989 Saleen Production Chart

Model	Price	Production
41 (hatchback)	$23,500	549*
44 (convertible)	$26,450	165
40 (coupe)	N/A	20
41 (hatchback SSC)	$36,500	161
Year Total		895

*Output includes 3 competition models.

1989 SALEEN SSC

1989 SALEEN SSC

On April 17, 1989 — the 25th birthday of Ford's Mustang — Saleen Autosport debuted its long-awaited SSC model. The SSC was a huge step forward for Saleen Autosport as a company because it was built around a 292-hp, 5.0-liter V-8 approved for sale by the Environmental Protection Agency in all 50 states. This was no small accomplishment for a small-volume automaker in 1989.

The SSC's interior was an altar where the marriage of luxury and performance took place, with leather FloFit seats and matching door panels coddling the lucky owner. The SSC speedometer registered 200 miles an hour, even though top speed was more realistically in the low-150 range. There was no back seat in the SSC because the area was taken up with 200 watts of Pioneer sound system, CD player and six speakers. A four-point interior chassis support system (known in the old, pre-lawsuit days as a "rollbar") further stiffened the Mustang platform.

Because of the incredible list of standard equipment, there were absolutely no options available. All 161 SSCs produced as 1989-only models were identical. All were white with white wheels and gray-and-white interiors. The only differences lay in running changes affected by component suppliers. For example, not all cars received the Momo steering wheel. Certifying, building, and selling a modified engine package made Saleen customers happy, but it also gave the company a broader product range that now included a constantly evolving "base" model as well as a high-end super car.

The attention Saleen received for his SSC helped take the focus away from Ford, which many Mustang fans felt were insulting their favorite car by not offering a special anniversary edition. The asking price for Saleen's "unofficial" 25th anniversary Mustang model was $36,500.

1989 SALEEN SSC 292-HP 5.0 V-8

SALEEN SSC POWER-TRAIN AND SUSPENSION

Conception of the SSC took place in 1988 when Saleen announced plans to produce a special 300-horsepower package to celebrate the company's upcoming fifth anniversary. That all-black "SA-5" (meaning Saleen Autosport 5th anniversary) never got past the prototype stage before it evolved into the SSC.

Saleen's modifications to the 5.0 included a 65mm throttle body (up from the stock Mustang's 60mm), revised intake plenum, enlarged cylinder head ports, wider rocker arm ratios, stainless steel tubular headers, heavy-duty cooling system, and Walker Dynomax mufflers.

A high-performance version of the Mustang's Borg-Warner T-5 transmission was installed behind the new power plant and controlled by a Hurst short-throw shifter. Standard 3.55:1 gears were housed in an Auburn "cone clutch" differential for ground-scorching acceleration.

Three-way Monroe Formula GA electronic cockpit-adjustable shock absorbers were quite an innovation at the time and Steve Saleen had to have them on his flagship SSC. Massive 245/50-16 General XP-2000Z rubber sat on the rear, with the slightly narrower front receiving 225/50-16Zs. SSC wheels were beautiful five-spoke, 16x8-inch DP models. Mechanically, the car either benefited from the stock Saleen inventory or, in most cases, went one better with all-new equipment.

Although the final horsepower rating of 292 fell short of Saleen's intended 300, the SSC was considered a hit in the Mustang world because it marked the first time since the 1960s that a small-volume manufacturer was able to legally sell a car powered by a modified engine.

1989 Saleen Engines			
Code	Engine	Power (hp)	Transmission
M	302-cid (5.0-liter) V-8	225	M5, A4
M	302-cid (5.0-liter) V-8 SSC	292	M5

1990 MUSTANG LX 5.0 HARDTOP

1990 MUSTANG

Federal regulations gave the Mustang its most important new equipment for 1990 in the form of a driver's side air bag and standard rear shoulder belts. Because of the steering wheel-mounted air bag, a tilt steering column was no longer available. Door panels now held map pockets, probably to make up for the now-missing console-mounted armrest.

Sedans, hatchbacks, and ragtops again came in LX and LX 5.0-liter series, with the hatchback and convertible available as GTs. The LX 5.0-liter models had the same beefy suspension and tires as the GT, while the GT package added spoilers and an air dam.

The LX 5.0 Sport models came in all three body styles, with prices starting at $12,107 for the coupe and reaching $17,681 for the convertible. The LX 5.0L came with the heftier suspension and bigger tires from the GT, but without the GT's spoilers and air dams.

The Mustang tradition was recognized in sales literature. It included passages such as, "Mustang, the first pony car, brought affordable sporty car performance and styling to every street and highway in America. And what it did best 25 years ago, it still does the best today." The factory built 128,189 of the 1990 Mustangs, making it the fifth most popular compact car sold in America despite a nearly 50 percent drop from the previous year.

1990 Production Chart			
Model	**Price**	**Weight**	**Production**
40 (notchback LX)	$9,638	2,634	*
41 (hatchback LX)	$10,144	2,634	*
44 (convertible LX)	$14,495	2,871	*
42 (hatchback GT)	$13,929	3,065	*
45 (convertible GT)	$18,303	3,213	*
Year Total			128,189*
* Ford reports total production of 22,503 notchbacks, 26,958 convertibles and 78,728 hatchbacks.			

1990 MUSTANG LIMITED EDITION

1990 LIMITED EDITION

There were 4,103 5.0-liter 1990 LX convertibles produced in Emerald Green with white interiors, 16-spoke wheels from the GT, and commemorative badges. Clear coat paint was now optional, as was leather interior trim for the V-8 hatchbacks.

Historians know them as the "7UP" cars because they were built as promotional giveaways for the 1990 National Collegiate Athletic Association finals. The public incorrectly labeled them "25th Anniversary" specials because of the timing of their release. Ford simply called them Limited Editions.

All Limited Editions were equipped with 5.0-liter V-8s, of which 2,743 were hooked to automatic transmissions and 1,360 were backed by five-speed manuals.

Ad lines:
225 Horses are Bound to Kick Something.

1990 Engines				
Code	Engine	Intake	Power (hp)	Transmission
A	140-cid SOHC 4	EFI	90	M5, A3
M	302-cid V-8	EFI	225	M5, A4

1990 SUPERCHARGED SALEEN CONVERTIBLE

1990 SALEEN

Steve Saleen became a household name by developing the Mustang into a world-class performance car, but America's recession in the late 1980s and early 1990s nearly consigned him to footnote status. Sales figures for the 1989 production made it look as though Saleen Autosport was poised to take its standard model and premium line to an even larger audience. That next level would have to wait a few years as a slow economy pulled the rug out from under the high-performance car market.

With the economy visibly slowing, Saleen worked against the odds to develop and improve his two well-loved products for 1990. It was the same "never quit" mindset that had won him the 1987 SCCA championship, and it would serve him well during the rough times.

The basic Mustang was not fundamentally different in 1990 — a driver's airbag and improved front suspension geometry being the only obvious changes. So it isn't surprising the standard Saleen was almost identical to the previous year's offering. The Racecraft suspension system now included variable rate front and rear coil springs (gone were the stiff, specific-rate units), Monroe Formula GP gas shocks all around, special strut mounting bearings, urethane sway bar pivot bushing, and high-performance alignment specs. Due to changes made by Ford, Saleen modified the shock tower brace this year.

The standard stereo was again a Pioneer AM/FM cassette unit with six speakers, graphic equalizer and a remote control. Other standard equipment included 225/50ZR-16 General XP-2000Z tires on American Racing rims (16 x 7 inches in front, 16 x 8 inches in rear), Monroe quad shocks, four-wheel disc brakes, Saleen aerodynamic kit, 170-mph speedometer, Hurst quick-ratio shifter, and articulated FloFit sport seats. New for 1990 were a "split" front air dam, two-piece rear wing and bolt-on subframe connectors.

The only options listed were the 3.55:1 limited-slip axle, Pioneer CD player and leather interior. Customers could make special requests such as automatic transmissions, sunroofs and certain aftermarket performance enhancements.

Only 243 standard Saleen Mustangs were built in 1990.

1990 SALEEN MUSTANG SC

1990 SALEEN SC

Saleen Autosport's development of the 1989 SSC's federally certified 5.0-liter V-8 was planned from the start to be the basis for a long line of premium-priced super cars from the company.

In 1990, the one-year-only SSC evolved into the "SC" where it continued giving Saleen enthusiasts power, handling, and appearance upgrades. Continuous improvements and changes to the aerodynamic body pieces, wheels and tires, and various other equipment proceeded deliberately during this period. Although the SC was lighter and more powerful (304 horsepower) than the SSC, only 13 of the hatchback-only models were built in 1990.

The slowing sales led Saleen to find creative ways to continue production, including the subcontracting of its conversion work to Cars & Concepts in St. Louis, Mo., in the middle of 1990. A California-based spin-off company, Saleen Parts Inc., assembled the SCs.

1990 Saleen Production Chart

Model	Price	Production
41 (hatchback)	$24,990	173
44 (convertible)	$29,390	62
40 (coupe)	$24,190	8
41 (hatchback SC)	$32,000	13
Year Total		256

1990 Saleen Engines

Code	Engine	Power (hp)	Transmission
M	302-cid (5.0-liter) V-8	225	M5, A4
M	302-cid (5.0-liter) V-8	304	M5

1991 MUSTANG 5.0 HATCHBACK

1991 MUSTANG

A new convertible top design looked crisper and fit lower in the 1991 Mustang storage well for a smoother profile when down. 1991 saw the base Mustang cross the $10,000 mark for the first time, thanks to a 2.9 to 3.3 percent sticker price increase. It is worth noting, however, that V-8 convertibles could be had for less than $20,000. The base coupe, hatchback, and convertible line had list prices from $10,157 to $16,222. Standard equipment included the overhead cam 2.3-liter four with electronic multi-point fuel injection, power front disc brakes (rear drums), five-speed manual overdrive transmission, and P195/75R-14 black sidewall all-season LX tires.

Interior changes added new cloth seat materials on the 2.3-liter LX models. Other improvements included vinyl door trim panel inserts added to power window-equipped units and an articulated sport seat standard on the LX 5.0-liter sedan. Options added for 1991 included cargo tie down net, front floor mats, graphic equalizer, 15-inch cast aluminum wheels with P205/65R-15 BSW tires (2.3-liter LX), and 14-inch styled road wheels.

Mustang production for model year 1991 totaled 98,737 units, a 1.7 percent share of the overall market (down from 2.1 percent the previous season). For 1991, 63 percent of all Mustangs, a total of 62,204 cars, had V-8s under their hoods and 36,533 had four-cylinder power plants.

1991 Production Chart			
Model	**Price**	**Weight**	**Production**
40 (notchback LX)	$10,157	2,759	*
41 (hatchback LX)	$10,663	2,824	*
44 (convertible LX)	$16,222	2,960	*
42 (hatchback GT)	$15,034	3,191	*
45 (convertible GT)	$19,864	3,327	*
Year Total			98,737*

* Ford reports total production of 19,447 notchbacks, 21,513 convertibles and 57,777 hatchbacks. Although not broken down by body, there were 24,428 GTs and 27,880 LX V-8s built this year.

1991 MUSTANG 5.0-LITER V-8 ENGINE

1991 POWERTRAINS

Although the 5.0-liter V-8 chugged into 1991 with its same 225 hp, the four-cylinder received a bump in power from 88 hp to 105 hp through a new head design that incorporated two spark plugs per cylinder.

The unchanged multi-point fuel-injected V-8, EPA figures were 18/25 with a five-speed and 17/24 with the automatic. The four-cylinder received a 21/28 (city/highway miles per gallon) EPA rating with the five-speed and 22/30 with automatic. These figures reflect the standard rear axle ratios.

Ad lines:
But I had to Grow Up to Get It.

1991 Engines				
Code	Engine	Intake	Power (hp)	Transmission
S	140-cid SOHC 4	EFI	105	M5, A3
E	302-cid V-8	EFI	225	M5, A4

1991-'93 MUSTANG 16-INCH ALLOY WHEEL

16-INCH ALLOY WHEEL

Both GT and LX 5.0-liter models received new, upsized 16-inch five-spoke aluminum wheels in 1991. Ford performed a slight modification to the plastic inner fender liners to increase clearance for the larger rim and the low-profile P225/55ZR-16 all-season Goodyear GT+4 performance tires that became standard on the LX 5.0-liter and optional on GT. Standard GT tires were P225/55ZR16 unidirectional Goodyear Gatorbacks.

Many V-8 Mustangs were shipped with P225/55ZR16 Michelin XGTZ4s when Goodyear's Gatorbacks were in short supply. There were no more changes in the wheel and tire combination through the end of 1993 production.

1991 SALEEN HATCHBACK

1991 SALEEN

Saleen kept production of its standard cars in St. Louis at the Cars & Concepts facility for the entirety of the 1991 model year, while SCs were assembled in Long Beach, Calif., by Saleen Performance Parts.

The company's Racecraft suspension system included variable rate front and rear coil springs, Monroe Formula GP gas shocks all around, special strut mounting bearings, urethane sway bar pivot bushing, and high-performance alignment specs. Standard features included 225/50ZR-16 General XP-2000Z tires on American Racing rims, Monroe quad shocks, four-wheel disc brakes, 170-mph speedometer, articulated FloFit sport seats, and a Saleen Mustang jacket.

Customers could make special requests such as automatic transmissions, sunroofs and certain aftermarket performance enhancements.

Participating Ford dealers were required to order cars for conversion with the following specs: LX hatchback, coupe or convertible, 5.0-liter V-8, five-speed manual transmission, 3.08:1 limited-slip axle, 225/60VR-15 tires, radio delete, Custom Equipment Group and rear window defogger.

The SC super car continued with few significant changes. With car sales continuing to decline throughout the industry, only 92 standard Saleen Mustangs and 10 SCs found new homes.

1991 Saleen Production Chart

Model	Price	Production
41 (hatchback)	$25,990	58
44 (convertible)	$29,990	30
40 (coupe)	$24,990	4
41 (hatchback SC)	$34,750	10
Year Total		102

1991 Saleen Engines

Code	Engine	Power (hp)	Transmission
E	302-cid (5.0-liter) V-8	225	M5, A4
E	302-cid (5.0-liter) V-8 SC	304	M5

1992 MUSTANG LX 5.0 HATCHBACK

1992 MUSTANG

Ford's plans for a major 1994 redesign meant there would be very few changes to the 1992-'93 Mustang package. The lack of any real improvements and a slow economy gave the marque its lowest sales level in history. As inflation continued to take its toll on the auto industry, the GT convertible had the dubious honor of being the first Mustang with a suggested retail price eclipsing $20,000, at $20,199. Base hardtops, hatchbacks, and convertibles ran from $10,215 to $16,899.

Standard equipment included the overhead cam 2.3-liter four with electronic fuel-injection, power front disc brakes (rear drums), five-speed manual overdrive transmission, and P195/75R-14 black sidewall all-season tires. All three body styles again came with LX or LX 5.0-liter series, with the hatchback and convertible available in GT trim. The base LX 5.0-liter Mustangs were priced from $13,422 to $19,644. The GT hatchback cost $15,243.

The 1992 Mustang received some body enhancements including color-keyed body side molding, bumper strips, a four-way power driver's seat option, and two new colors, Bimini Blue and Calypso Green. When all was said and done, the 1992 Mustang had a 79,280-unit model year, making it the fifth most popular compact car in the United States. Production was split almost evenly between four-cylinder models (36,307 made) and V-8s (36,893 built).

1992 Production Chart			
Model	**Price**	**Weight**	**Production**
40 (notchback LX)	$10,215	2,775	*
41 (hatchback LX)	$10,721	2,834	*
44 (convertible LX)	$16,899	2,996	*
42 (hatchback GT)	$15,243	3,144	*
45 (convertible GT)	$20,199	3,365	*
Year Total			79,280*

* Ford reports total production of 15,717 notchbacks, 23,470 convertibles and 40,093 hatchbacks. Although not broken down by body, there were 20,445 GTs and 19,131 LX V-8s built this year.

1992½ MUSTANG LIMITED EDITION

1992½ LIMITED EDITION

Following the success of its all-green line of 1990 Limited Edition Mustangs, Ford built 2,019 5.0-liter LX convertibles in Vibrant Red as a mid-year attention getter.

These "Summer Special" models were available with either the four-speed automatic or five-speed manual transmissions, and could be ordered with any optional Mustang equipment. The cosmetic package included the unique red paint; color-keyed body parts such as moldings, mirrors and windshield frame; a white leather interior with black piping accents; and 16-inch five-spoke GT wheels coated in opal pearlescent paint.

The red Limited Edition marked the first time Ford installed a rear spoiler and integrated CHMSL on one of its LX convertibles. Conversions for this small run of convertibles was handled by Cars and Concepts in Michigan, the company responsible for turning Mustang notchbacks into ragtops for Ford.

The basic Limited Edition package added $850 to the cost of a 5.0 LX convertible, which set the car's retail price at $22,727.

Ad lines:
Go Ahead, Make Your Day.

1992 Engines				
Code	Engine	Intake	Power (hp)	Transmission
S	140-cid SOHC 4	EFI	105	M5, A3
E	302-cid V-8	EFI	225	M5, A4

1992 SALEEN MUSTANG CONVERTIBLE

1992 SALEEN

For Saleen fans, 1992 looked like the year the company would be forced to close its doors due to excruciatingly slow sales and a sluggish high-performance car market. Steve Saleen introduced several improvements to his 1992 line of Mustangs.

A new 17-inch wheel design gave the Saleen package a much-needed visual pickup. The 17-inch Stern wheels measured eight inches wide in front and nine inches in the rear, with Z-rated B.F. Goodrich Comp T/A radials all around. Saleen also returned to a single-piece rear wing after two years of an unpopular bi-level design.

Once again, the Racecraft suspension system included variable rate front and rear coil springs, Monroe Formula GP gas shocks all around, special strut mounting bearings, urethane sway bar pivot bushing, and high-performance alignment specs. Standard stereo equipment was again a Pioneer AM/FM cassette unit with six speakers, graphic equalizer and a remote control. Other standard features included Monroe quad shocks, four-wheel disc brakes, Saleen aerodynamic kit, and new-for-'92 articulated sport seats.

Options listed by the factory were the 3.55:1 limited-slip axle, Pioneer CD player and leather interior. Customers could request automatic transmissions, sunroofs and certain aftermarket performance enhancements.

Saleen introduced a "Spyder" convertible package featuring a soft tonneau cover that turned the rear seats into a convenient storage area. Saleen began offering a Vortech supercharger as an option, and Recaro came on board to supply its legendary seats.

Only 17 standard Saleens were sold in 1992, and no SCs were built. When Cars & Concepts closed its St. Louis plant at the end of 1991, Saleen moved all of its Mustang production to the Long Beach-based Saleen Performance Parts for 1992.

1992 Saleen Production Chart		
Model	**Price**	**Production**
41 (hatchback)	$26,990	12
44 (convertible)	$30,990	5
Year Total		17

1993 MUSTANG LX 5.0 HARDTOP

1993 MUSTANG

The bad news for 1993 was that the Mustang V-8 lost 20 horsepower. The good news was that it was only a paper loss. Ford made no modifications to the 5.0-liter in the year before introducing its redesigned Mustang, but explained the theoretical power deficit as being the result of a new system for measurement on the dynamometer.

The 14-year-old "Fox" Mustang went into its seventh and final year with only small changes distinguishing it from the previous year. It came in LX, LX 5.0-liter, and GT form. Base LX models, equipped with the 2.3-liter four-cylinder engine, stickered for $10,719 for the sedan, $11,224 for the hatchback, and $17,548 for the convertible. Standard LX equipment included a driver's side air bag; a heavy-duty 75-ampere alternator; a heavy-duty 58-ampere battery; power brakes with front discs and rear drums; color-keyed front and rear bumper rub strips; full carpeting; a digital clock; a center console with armrest; the 2.3-liter four-cylinder engine;

a fuel cap tether; tinted glass; a color-keyed cloth headliner; dual horns; luxury sound insulation; dome, cargo area, under hood, ashtray, and glove box lamps; dual, manual remote-controlled rearview mirrors; dual covered visor mirrors; color-keyed body side moldings; an AM/FM radio with electronic tuning and four speakers; reclining low-back bucket seats; a front stabilizer bar; power steering; body side paint stripes; a tachometer; a five-speed manual transmission; a trip odometer; cloth upholstery; a headlight warning chime; finned wheel covers; intermittent windshield wipers; and P195/75R-14 steel-belted radial all-season black sidewall tires.

The GT hatchback ($15,747) and convertible ($20,848) also had a front air dam; fog lights; color-keyed, flared rocker panel moldings; no body side paint stripes; and performance tires of the same size as LX 5.0-liter models. LX 5.0-liter models were priced at $13,926 for the sedan, $14,710 for the hatchback, and $20,293 for the convertible.

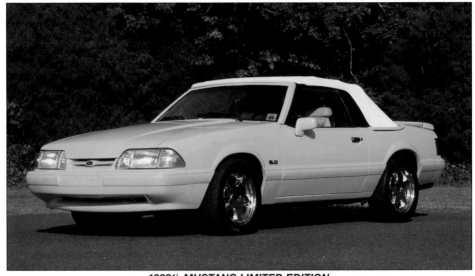

1993½ MUSTANG LIMITED EDITION

1993½ LIMITED EDITION

For 1993, Ford produced a mid-year Limited Edition with two different trim packages and colors.

An extra $1,488 bought 5.0-liter LX convertible buyers a monochromatic Canary Yellow paint scheme with chrome 16-inch aluminum rims and color-keyed top, bringing the vehicle's base price to $22,221.

More sedate Mustang buyers could pony up $976 to create an Oxford White Limited Edition with a white interior and top, for a total MSRP of $21,709.

Identical rear spoilers with integrated CHMSLs (center high-mounted stoplights) were fitted to each model, and both received color-matching mirror housings, molding and windshield surrounds. Interior upgrades included headrests with embossed pony emblems and decorative black floor mats.

The $512 price difference between packages was due to the cost of chroming the yellow car's wheels.

1993 Production Chart

Model	Price	Weight	Production
40 (notchback LX)	$10,719	2,751	*
41 (hatchback LX)	$11,224	2,812	*
44 (convertible LX)	$17,548	2,973	*
42 (hatchback GT)	$15,747	3,144	*
45 (convertible GT)	$20,848	3,365	*
Year Total			114,228*

* Ford reports total production of 24,851 notchbacks, 27,300 convertibles and 62,077 hatchbacks. Although not broken down by body, there were 26,101 GTs and 22,902 LX V-8s built this year. Figure for hatchbacks includes 4,993 SVT Cobras and 107 SVT Cobra R models.

1993 Engines

Code	Engine	Intake	Power (hp)	Transmission
S	140-cid SOHC 4	EFI	105	M5, A3
E	302-cid V-8	EFI	205	M5, A4
D	302-cid V-8 Cobra	EFI	235	M5

1993 SVT COBRA

1993 SVT COBRA

The 1993 SVT Cobra was a going-away present for the 14-year-old Fox-based Mustang platform. It was a beefed-up bon voyage party that only 5,100 special guests could enjoy. Ford's Special Vehicle Team (SVT) was created to raise the Mustang's performance bar by producing a limited run of factory-blessed super cars. Both SVT and the Special Vehicle Engineering (SVE) groups were formed late in 1991 to bring a new line of upscale high-performance products to Ford dealerships. SVT handled the marketing, training, and customer-relations chores. SVE was devoted to developing and building the final product. In February of 1992, it was announced that the first two SVT vehicles would be introduced as 1993 models—a fast turnaround!

Because Ford's full-size pickup line was the most popular in its class, SVT decided that a short-wheelbase F-150 with a 351-cid/240-hp V-8 would establish the company as the leader in the small performance truck market. Following the "Lightning" would be a hopped-up version of the Mustang built using many of the go-fast parts already sold through Ford's existing dealer network.

When SVT announced it would call its Mustang "Cobra," longtime enthusiasts feared the promised Camaro-killer might turn out to be just another tape-and-stripe job. The coiled snake emblem had meant little since Carroll Shelby stopped using it in 1967. The 1976-78 Mustang II Cobra II, 1978 King Cobra and anemic Cobra models of the early 1980s had de-fanged the hooded serpent.

Fears were relieved when the Cobra hit showrooms mid-year, with enthusiast publications and Mustang fans declaring it to be a true successor to the hallowed name.

1993 Cobra Production Chart

Model	Price	Weight	Production
42 (hatchback Cobra)	$18,505	3,255	4,993
42 (hatchback Cobra R)	$25,692	3,195	107
Year Total			5,100*

* SVT reports color breakdown for 1993 Cobras as 1,882 Vibrant Red Clearcoat, 1,854 Black, 1,355 Teal Metallic and 9 Vibrant Red.

1993 SVT COBRA 5.0-LITER V-8

COBRA DRIVE TRAIN AND SUSPENSION

The 1993 Cobra hit showrooms as a hatch-back only; its sole power plant offering was a 235-hp version of Ford's strong-but-old 5.0-liter V-8. The 30 hp boost was due to new upper and lower intake manifold designs, revised "GT40" heads with larger intake and exhaust ports, larger valves and revised rocker arms. Throttle body and mass air sensor size were increased to 70mm and 65mm, respectively, for better flow, and a different cam spec was used. The intake manifold was a special two-piece GT40 design cast from aluminum. Smaller crank and water pump pulleys were installed, an old hot rod trick. Block and heads were cast in iron. Redline for the Cobra V-8 was a giddy 6,000 rpm.

Borg-Warner's T-5 transmission was similar to the stock Mustang component, but improved with phosphate-coated gears and stronger bearings. A short-throw shifter helped the enthusiastic driver make positive gear changes, and the 8.8-inch limited-slip differential was fitted with 3.08:1 cogs. The driveshaft was made of steel.

SVT installed four-wheel disc brakes on every Cobra it sold for 1993. The 10.84-inch front rotors were vented, with single-piston calipers. The 10.07-inch rears were also vented and wore calipers actuated by single pistons. Goodyear 245/45ZR-17 Eagle uni-directional tires were mounted on Cobra-unique 17 x 7.5-inch seven-blade alloy rims. The low-profile tires and lower body ride height gave the Cobra great handling.

Surprisingly, the suspension was set up to ride softer than Ford's stock GT as part of SVT's "controlled compliance" philosophy. Front components included modified MacPherson struts, with separate springs on the lower arms, 400/505-pounds-per-inch variable rate coil springs and a 28.5mm stabilizer bar. Underneath the rear of the car was a rigid axle, upper and lower trailing arms, two leading hydraulic links, 160 pounds-per-inch constant-rate coil springs, shock absorbers and a stabilizer bar.

1993 Cobra Engine			
Code	Engine	Power (hp)	Transmission
D	302-cid (5.0-liter) EFI V-8	235	M5

1993 SVT COBRA R

1993 SVT COBRA R

It was common knowledge by mid-1993 that the Mustang was due for a major re-design, but Ford and SVT wanted the Fox era to end on a high note and draw attention away from General Motors' new 275-hp Camaros and Firebirds. Rather than rest on the immediate success of the Cobra, SVT decided to send the "Fox" platform to its final resting place in style with a competition model. The Cobra "R" was released in the summer of 1993 to improve Ford's status in the International Motor Sport Association (IMSA) Firestone Grand Sport Series and Sports Car Club of America (SCCA) World Challenge Class B Series.

Race-ready Koni shock absorbers, an en- gine cooling kit, upgraded brakes, and five-lug wheels were added to the package, while non-necessities such as air conditioning, the back seat, sound deadening and auxiliary lights were removed to save weight. Special blacked-out wheels with three twin-spoke arms and chromed hub covers were installed.

While the regular Cobra was available in Performance Red, Teal or Black, the R only came in Performance Red. SVT's goal of selling 5,000 Cobras was all but met by the end of the model year, with 4,993 of the $18,505 hatch-backs going to new owners. An additional 107 "R" models were sold for $25,692 apiece.

1993 SALEEN MUSTANG

1993 SALEEN

Steve Saleen's operation hit bottom in 1992, with only 17 of the special Mustangs constructed. As the company struggled to remain afloat, luck tossed a life preserver in the form of a recovering economy and a relationship with Tim Allen when the "Home Improvement" star arranged a meeting with its creator and requested a one-off model built around his man-humor mantra of "more power!"

That "R-R-R" model, brought the company an enormous amount of much-needed attention. The 576-hp 5.0-liter V-8 Saleen built for the all-white hatchback featured a balanced and blueprinted block, ported and polished aluminum heads, Saleen-spec upper and lower intake manifold, 65mm throttle body, 1.72:1 aluminum roller rocker arms, 38 lbs./hr. fuel injectors, ceramic headers, and a Vortech "B-trim" supercharger pumping out 13.5 pounds per square inch. Transferring the "caR-R-R's" massive power to the ground was a Tremec five-speed transmission, aluminum driveshaft, and an Auburn cone-clutch differential with 3.55:1 gears. At Allen's request, huge brake discs all around and four-piston calipers kept the horsepower from getting the comedian in trouble on the racetrack or street.

Saleen's two lines of Mustangs–the "standard" and SC–continued much the same as before. The Racecraft suspension system included variable rate front and rear coil springs, Saleen/Racecraft gas shocks all around, special strut mounting bearings, urethane sway bar pivot bushing, and high-performance alignment specs. The standard stereo was again a Pioneer AM/FM cassette unit with six speakers, graphic equalizer and a remote control. Other standard equipment included 235/45ZR-17 and 245/45ZR-17 B.F. Goodrich tires on Stern rims (17 x 8 inches in front, 17 x 9 inches in rear), Saleen/Racecraft quad shocks, four-wheel disc brakes, Saleen aerodynamic kit, 170-mph speedometer, Hurst quick-ratio shifter and articulated Recaro sport seats.

Production for 1993 was slow, but a remarkable improvement over the previous year. Saleen sold 87 of its base Mustang packages (23 of which had Vortech superchargers), five SCs and nine supercharged SA-10 models commemorating Saleen's 10th year in business. For 1993 only, it was possible to order the SC as a convertible; three were sold.

1993 SALEEN MUSTANG SA-10

1993 SALEEN SA-10

Saleen was a reinvigorated company in 1993. It was preparing to close the book on the "Fox" series and developing a major surprise for the next year based on Ford's redesigned Mustang. With optimism and buyer interest running high again, Saleen produced a limited run of nine SA-10 models to celebrate the company's 10th anniversary.

Looking unlike any other Ford or Saleen Mustang, the SA-10 hatchback, available only in black with yellow trim, was powered by a modified and supercharged version of the 5.0-liter V-8. The company encouraged each buyer to customize the car by consulting the Saleen Performance Parts catalog when ordering, which resulted in nine unique combinations.

The special model featured many high-performance pieces first offered on the SSC and SC, such as sub-frame connectors, chassis support braces, a rear shock tower brace and a Panhard rod. The SA-10 was to be the last of the 5.0-liter Saleen Mustangs as the company's 1994 offerings would be based around a 5.8-liter/351-cid V-8.

1993 Saleen Production Chart

Model	Price	Production
41 (hatchback)	$27,490	56 *
44 (convertible)	$31,690	30
40 (coupe)	$26,790	1
41 (hatchback SC)	$39,990	2
44 (convertible SC)	$44,490	3
41 (hatchback SA-10)	$37,995	9
41 (hatchback R-R-R)	N/A	1
Year Total		102

* Output includes one competition model.

1993 Saleen Engines

Code	Engine	Power (hp)	Transmission
E	302-cid (5.0-liter) V-8	205	M5, A4
E	302-cid (5.0-liter) V-8	450	M5, A4

1994 MUSTANG GT

1994 MUSTANG

Introduced on Oct. 15, 1993, as a 1994 model, the new Mustang was essentially a high-tech updating of the 1979 "Fox" chassis, but with only a few carryover components buried deep within the platform.

Because chassis stiffness had always been a weakness of the 1979 through 1993 generation (especially when the unplanned convertible came along), engineering goals for rigidity on the new platform were set quite high. New techniques were used to achieve stiffness in the coupe, including bonding the windshield and backlight to their frames with a rigid urethane adhesive and by enlarging certain box sections as the rocker panels and roof rails. On the GT V-8 models, the structure was further improved with the addition of a bolt-in brace tying the front strut towers and cowl/firewall together — a trick Mustang modifiers had been using since the mid-1980s to get less flex out of the car under extreme cornering applications.

Aerodynamic headlights sat on either side of a curved grille cavity that, when combined with the smooth bumper cover and integrated air dam, provided a pleasant, smiling face. Modern production techniques did a better job of creating a coupe with a gently radiused top — the curvy, almost dome-like top really complemented the rounder body. Three-element taillights (lying horizontal on the 1994, unlike the 1965's vertical units) recalled some of the Mustang's early heritage and contributed to the impression of great body width when viewed from directly behind. A classic twin-cockpit theme ran throughout the new interior.

The 1994 Mustang measured 2.4 inches longer (181.5 inches bumper-to-bumper) than the first "Fox" car. Wheelbase increased between the two models by 0.9 inches to a total of 101.3. The most striking dimension change was in the width, wherein the 1994 was a muscular 71.9 inches compared to the slab-sided 1979's 69.1 inches. The 1994 Mustang's roofline was 1.4 inches higher than the 1979 at 52.9 inches.

1994-'95 MUSTANG GT 17-INCH WHEEL

1994 MUSTANG POWERTRAINS AND SUSPENSION

The same torquey 3.8-liter 145-hp V-6 that was already serving in Ford's Taurus, Thunderbird, and Lincoln Continental replaced the Mustang's four-cylinder and increased horsepower by 38 percent for 1994. The legendary 5.0-liter H.O. V-8 was boosted to 215 hp at 4200 rpm courtesy of a low-profile intake manifold (to fit under the more steeply raked hood) and pistons cast in hypereutectic aluminum alloy.

Four-wheel disc brakes were applied to factory Mustangs for the first time in 1994 on both base and GT cars, with ABS an extra-cost option.

Buyers of the base V-6 cars received 15-inch steel wheels with plastic covers and 205/65-15 all-season black sidewall Goodyear Eagle GA tires. Those tires could be mounted on three-spoke, 15-inch alloy wheels. Standard GT wheels were five-spoke, 16-inch rims wearing 225/55-16 Firestone Firehawk rubber. An optional upgrade for the GT was a set of three-spoke 17-inchers shod with 245/45-17 Goodyear Eagle GTs.

The all-new Mustang readily won Motor Trend magazine's "Car of the Year" award, and it became the Indianapolis 500 pace car for the third time since 1964.

1994 Production Chart

Model	Price	Weight	Production
40 (coupe)	$13,355	3,055	42,883
44 (convertible)	$20,150	3,193	18,333
42 (coupe GT)	$17,270	3,258	30,592
45 (convertible GT)	$21,960	3,414	25,381
Year Total			123,198

* Figure includes 5,009 SVT Cobra coupes and 1,000 convertibles.

1994 Engines

Code	Engine	Intake	Power (hp)	Transmission
4	232-cid V-6	EFI	145	M5, A4
E	302-cid V-8	EFI	215	M5, A4
D	302-cid V-8 Cobra	EFI	240	M5

MACH 460 STEREO OPTION

MACH 460 STEREO

Ford's Mustang design team knew its young target audience liked its car stereos to be powerful and loaded on the bottom end, so putting together a top-of-the-line sound system to rival the "boom trucks" so prevalent in southern California became a top priority.

The company's electronics division, the creators of several high-quality JBL Gold stereo packages for Lincoln, put together 14 specialized components to be known collectively as the Mach 460 option. The user interface part of the package was the digital tuner/cassette player, which fed its high-tech signal to a four-channel amplifier, two subwoofers, two mid-range tweeters and two woofers.

The woofers were located on the package trays in coupes, but moved lower into the rear quarter panel enclosures in convertibles.

For only $375 over the cost of the base stereo, a 1994 Mustang buyer could surround himself with music quality as fine as anything on the market.

The 1994 Mustang was also the first Ford to offer a dealer-installed mini-disc sound system.

1994 SVT COBRA

1994 SVT COBRA

The Cobra was updated to the "SN-95" platform for 1994 with a lower hood line, higher deck lid and gentle, curved roof. Distinguishing the higher-priced Cobra from the GT was a new bumper fascia sporting round auxiliary lights (the GT lights were smaller and rectangular). Crystal clear, European-style reflector headlamps gave the Cobra the edge for nighttime high-performance driving, and the pedestal-mounted rear spoiler had an LED brake light built in. Emblems depicting coiled snakes replaced the GT fender badges.

Interior design touches included a steering wheel embossed with the word "Cobra," Cobra-unique floor mats and white-faced gauges (including a 160-mph speedometer). A little-noticed upgrade is the switch from steel to magnesium for the front seat cushion frames.

The heart of the beast, the 5.0-liter V-8, enjoyed some computer tinkering that boosted it to 240 hp and 285 lbs.-ft. of torque. The GT used the Thunderbird 5.0-liter manifold to fit under the steeply sloped hood, but SVT decided to retain the taller 1993 piece for more power. In order to fit everything under the hood, the strut tower-to-cowl brace was removed.

Four-wheel disc brakes with a five-lug pattern became the standard Mustang setup for 1994. The Cobra used larger ABS-equipped discs assigned to handle the extra horsepower. Front-vented discs measured 13.0 inches in diameter and were fitted with twin-piston "Cobra"-embossed calipers. Rears were vented discs measuring 11.65 inches. Goodyear 255/45ZR-17 uni-directional Eagle GS-Cs were mounted on five-spoke, 17 x 8-inch alloy rims, and a 17-inch mini spare was tucked away in the trunk.

1994 Cobra Production Chart

Model	Price	Weight	Production
42 (coupe Cobra)	$20,765	3,365	5,009
45 (convertible Cobra)	$26,845	3,567	1,000
Year Total			6,009*

* SVT reports color breakdown for 2,908 Rio Red coupes, 1,000 Rio Red convertibles, 1,795 Black coupes and 1,306 Crystal White coupes.

1994 SVT COBRA PACE CAR CONVERTIBLE

1994 SVT COBRA PACE CAR

Ford chose to show off its new top-line Cobra convertible by having one pace the 1994 Indianapolis 500. Three cars were modified by Jack Roush for heavy-duty "real" pace car chores, while SVT turned out 1,000 Rio Red replicas with Saddle leather interiors and Saddle tops. As with most pace car knock-offs, decals were shipped to the dealers inside the cars (not on them) and left to the buyer's discretion to install.

The three race-day duty pace cars were modified at Roush's shop in Allen Park, Mich., with specially "tweaked" four-speed automatic transmissions, 15-gallon racing fuel cells, heavier rear springs (to accommodate the weight of television camera equipment), a Halon fire-extinguisher system, a rollbar with 50,000-watt strobe lights built in and special lights in the rear spoiler.

Regular 1994 Cobra standard equipment included dual airbags, articulated sport seats (with four-way power driver's seat), premium stereo, Power Equipment Group, rear window defroster, speed control, Cobra floor mats and dual illuminated visor mirrors. Regular Cobra options for 1994 included leather interior, remote keyless entry system and the Mach 460/CD equipment. The pace car replica included all of these options as standard.

1994 Cobra Engine			
Code	Engine	Power (hp)	Transmission
D	302-cid (5.0-liter) EFI V-8	240	M5

1994 SALEEN MUSTANG S-351

1994 SALEEN S-351

Ford and Saleen Mustang sales had been slowing to a crawl in the early 1990s, the result of a body style that had overstayed its welcome by several years. When Ford Motor Co. debuted an all-new design late in 1993, the eyes of the Mustang world looked toward Steve Saleen's shop in California. In April at Charlotte Motor Speedway, the Mustang's 30th anniversary show introduced the S-351, a premium-priced super car that took the previous SSC and SC concepts to the next level.

Powered by an SVT Lightning-derived 351-cid 371-hp V-8 built and EPA-certified by Saleen Performance, the S-351 had the highest Saleen-unique content of any car to date. In most cases from 1994 through its final year of production in 1999, V-6 coupes and convertibles were delivered to the new Saleen factory in Irvine, Calif., then were stripped to bare shells (except for certain components such as the dash). A handful were converted from GTs, but there is no discernible difference between the two as a Saleen.

The upscale SR model was a barely legal version of the S-351 that dressed a Vortech-supercharged coupe or convertible in FIA Group

A competition clothing, including a dual-plane rear wing, carbon-fiber hood and scooped body side enhancements. The SR benefited from a rear race tray that replaced the back seat, four-point rollbar, four-point safety harness and racing Recaro seats. With its 351-cid supercharged V-8 rated at 480 hp, no one could say the SR was "all-show, no-go." The standard S-351 could also be ordered.

Both the S-351 and SR convertibles could be ordered as "Speedsters," a package that featured a rollbar-like "sport bar" and a hard tonneau cover.

With only a few months of real production time in 1994, Saleen dealers managed to sell 29 V-6 Sports, 44 S-351s and two SRs. The successful launch calmed fears that Saleen Autosport had gone the way of Shelby American.

1994 Saleen Production Chart		
Model	**Price**	**Production**
40-42 (coupe S-351)	$34,990	30
44-45 (convertible S-351)	$40,990	14
40 (coupe SR)	$45,990	2
Year Total		46

1994 SALEEN S-351 5.8-LITER SUPERCHARGED V-8

1994 S-351 POWERTRAIN AND SUSPENSION

Steve Saleen's custom-built and EPA-certified S-351 V-8 produced its 371 horsepower through the use of high-performance cylinder heads with bigger valves; hydraulic roller camshaft and lifters; 65mm throttle body; 77mm mass air sensor, and a slew of other high-tech goodies. The unique power plant was then installed on relocated motor mounts (one inch rearward and one inch lower than stock) and entirely rewired to a new EEC-IV engine management system. Just about every part of the S-351 was replaced or massaged during a period of 120 hours, which made the coupe's $34,990 asking price ($40,990 for the convertible) quite remarkable.

The stock 235/40-18 (front) and 245/40-18 (rear) B.F. Goodrich Comp T/A radials could be upgraded to Dunlop SP8000s measuring 255/40-18 and 285/40-18. Need more power?

The S-351 could be outfitted with any number of accessories, unlike the "no options" SSC of 1989. A dozen Saleen buyers opted for the Vortech supercharger option. Greater acceleration could be dialed in with a 3.55:1 rear axle. If stopping was as important as going, larger 13-inch brake discs could be ordered.

1994 Saleen Engines			
Code	**Engine**	**Power (hp)**	**Transmission**
4	232-cid (3.8-liter) V-6*	145	M5, A4
E	302-cid (5.0-liter) V-8*	215	M5, A4
N/A	351-cid (5.8-liter) V-8**	371	M5
N/A	351-cid (5.8-liter) V-8 super**	480	M5

* Removed from Saleen S-351s during conversion.
** Actual powertrains used in S-351 production.

1994 SALEEN SPORT V-6

1994 SALEEN V-6 SPORT

Every few years an automaker comes out with a genuinely good idea that, unfortunately, never quite finds enough willing buyers to sustain production. Ford's SVO Mustang and Merkur models and Pontiac's Fiero (with V-6) were steps in the right direction the public was not ready to take, but that many revere as "classics" now.

The same status should be accorded Saleen Performance's V-6 Sport, a model that combined traditional Saleen equipment with a less-expensive power plant. Boosted by a supercharger announced as standard equipment (but only a few were sold that way), the Sport's 3.8-liter V-6 was rated at 220 hp, just a bit more power than the heavier 5.0-liter V-8, and benefited from Race-craft suspension tuning, 17 x 8-inch wheels, and Saleen aerodynamic body pieces. A short-throw Hurst shifter and leather-grained shift knob were the only interior modifications.

With a window sticker of less than $22,000, the V-6 Sport (official name: V-6 Sport by Steve Saleen) was in the same price range as a loaded GT Mustang, but without the super-high insurance premium. The car was aimed at young buyers looking for performance, but that need was being filled in 1994 almost exclusively by imported models. Only 29 V-6 Sports were built, none of which were given Saleen-specific serial numbers, and the model was discontinued at the end of the year.

1995 MUSTANG GT

1995 MUSTANG

1995 was significant as the final year for the venerable 5.0-liter V-8 that had served the Mustang well since its introduction in 1968. Purists were cautiously awaiting the Five-Oh's replacement — a 4.6-liter, overhead cam version of Ford's new "modular" family.

Catering to 5.0-liter fans on a budget, Ford offered a GTS model that was essentially a GT without the sports seats, rear spoiler, and fog lamps. It did include the GT's standard 16-inch, five-spoke alloy wheels. The base Mustang continued to be offered with the 3.8-liter V-6. Ford's removable hardtop option for the convertible was quietly dropped from all sales literature.

The base coupe listed for $14,330; the base convertible, $20,795; the GTS coupe, $16,910; the GT coupe, $17,905; the GT convertible, $22,595; the Cobra coupe, $21,300; and the Cobra convertible topped the pile at $25,605. Sales were up in the second year of the new design, with a total of 185,986 units sold. That number included 137,722 coupes and 48,264 convertibles.

1995 Production Chart

Model	Price	Weight	Production
40 (coupe)	$14,330	3,077	*
44 (convertible)	$20,795	3,257	*
42 (coupe GT)	$17,905	3,280	*
45 (convertible GT)	$22,595	3,451	*
42 (coupe GTS)	$16,910	3,246	*
Year Total			185,986*

* Ford reports total production of 137,722 coupes, 48,264 convertibles, 4,005 SVT Cobra coupes, 1,003 Cobra convertibles and 250 Cobra R models.

1995 Engines

Code	Engine	Intake	Power (hp)	Transmission
4	232-cid V-6	EFI	145	M5, A4
E	302-cid V-8	EFI	215	M5, A4
D	302-cid V-8 Cobra	EFI	240	M5
C	351-cid V-8 Cobra R	EFI	300	M5

1995 SVT COBRA CONVERTIBLE WITH REMOVABLE HARDTOP

1995 SVT COBRA

SVT can perhaps be forgiven for only making minimal changes to its 1995 model, considering how successful efforts had been to create a first-rate super-Mustang! The only noticeable improvement was the permanent addition of a convertible to the lineup this year. It was only available in Black, with a Black leather interior and Black top. Coupe colors were restricted to Rio Red, Crystal White, and Black.

Under the hood, the powerful 240 hp 5.0-liter was unchanged, but an identification label was placed on the driver-side valve cover pro-claiming the Cobra's limited production status. After 28 years of nearly uninterrupted service to the Mustang, the pushrod 302 was being retired. Both the Cobra and GT would receive new "modular" V-8s in 1996. Regular Cobra standard equipment included dual airbags, articulated sport seats (with four-way power driver's seat), premium stereo, Power Equipment Group, rear window defroster, speed control, Cobra floor mats and dual illuminated visor mirrors. Options for 1995 included leather interior, remote keyless entry system and the Mach 460/CD equipment.

1995 Cobra Production Chart			
Model	**Price**	**Weight**	**Production**
42 (coupe Cobra)	$21,300	3,365	4,005
45 (convertible Cobra)	$25,605	3,567	1,003
42 (coupe Cobra R)	$35,499*	3,280	250
Year Total			5,258**
* Price does not include $2,100 gas guzzler tax. ** SVT reports color breakdown for 1,447 Rio Red coupes, 1,433 Black coupes, 1,003 Black convertibles and 1,125 Crystal White coupes.			

1995 SVT COBRA R

1995 SVT COBRA R

Since demand for the 1993 Cobra R had far exceeded the 100-car run, SVT increased availability of the 1995 version to 250 units. Many of the first Rs had gone straight to collectors' garages (bypassing the racetracks), so Ford insisted that sales of the '95 would be made only to licensed, active competitors in the SCCA and IMSA series.

The second-generation Cobra R signified a new high-water mark for late-model Mustang performance; not since 1973 had a Mustang been available with 351 cubic inches of small-block V-8. Since the standard Cobra's 5.0-liter/302-cid V-8 and R-model's 351-cid V-8 were part of the same "family," emissions certification was easier than if a different power plant had been chosen. A Ford marine block formed the basis for the super V-8, with a special camshaft, aluminum alloy pistons, forged steel connecting rods, GT40 heads and lower intake and specially designed upper intake manifold making up most of the performance gains. Visually topping off the package was a "5.8 Liter Cobra" plate on the intake manifold. The greater displacement pro-

duced 300 hp and 365 lbs.-ft. of torque.

SVT installed a beefier Tremec five-speed and 3.27:1 rear axle gears for neck-snapping acceleration. The R was stripped of unnecessary components, including the air conditioning system, radio, rear seat, some soundproofing materials and fog lamps. Suspension components included Eibach springs, Koni adjustable shocks, firmer bushings, five-spoke wheels measuring 17 x 9 inches and 255/45-17 B.F. Goodrich Comp T/As contributing to the competition-level handling. Other race-oriented pieces included a fiberglass hood, 20-gallon fuel cell and radiators for engine oil and power steering fluid. All 250 cars were painted Crystal White and fitted with the Saddle cloth interiors.

1995 Cobra Engines			
Code	Engine	Power (hp)	Transmission
D	302-cid (5.0-liter) EFI V-8	240	M5
C	351-cid (5.8-liter) EFI V-8	300	M5

1995 SVT COBRA REMOVABLE HARDTOP

1995 COBRA REMOVABLE HARDTOP

At the introduction of the SN-95 platform in 1994, Ford made quite a show of an optional removable hardtop for its convertible. Pictures taken before Job One reveal clear man-size plastic cutouts in the act of lifting a hardtop from the new Mustang as amazed onlookers gasp their approval. Unfortunately, the vendor Ford contracted to build the complicated piece had trouble delivering the product on time, which delayed availability of the option until the 1995 model year. Ford made the decision to introduce the hardtop to the production line by way of the Cobra, but stopped taking orders for the $1,825 option soon after.

Only 499 of the special tops were made, supposedly Cobras accounting for the majority of models so equipped. (Unfortunately for Mustang owners looking to retrofit their convertibles with the removable top, it can't be done without major, expensive modifications to the car.)

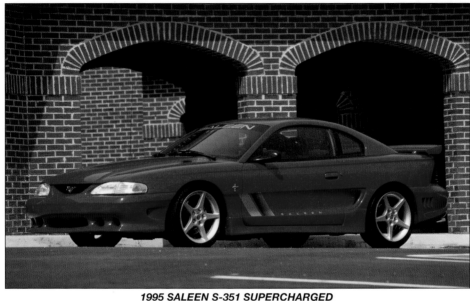

1995 SALEEN S-351 SUPERCHARGED

1995 SALEEN S-351

After launching the first truly new design in a decade the previous year, Saleen Performance was content to rest on its sporty laurels for 1995. Engine development continued as the company experimented with different fuel injector settings and added O-rings to its 351-cid V-8 engines being built for supercharger applications. The advertised horsepower output remained at 371 (standard) or 480 (supercharged), and both engines were hooked to a heavy-duty Tremec five-speed transmission and a stock rear axle gear ratio of 3.27:1.

The 1995 S-351 suspension included Racecraft struts and shocks, variable-rate coil springs, urethane sway bar bushings and caster/camber plates.

Steve Saleen and comedian Tim Allen combined forces to create the Saleen/Allen RRR Speedlab race team in 1995. They started the season with three cars, each equipped with a 580-hp aluminum-block 351 with competition fuel-injection and a Hewland five-speed manual transmission. Experiencing typical freshman blues, Saleen/Allen only managed to win the final race of the season at Sears Point.

1995 Saleen Production Chart

Model	Price	Production
40-42 (coupe S-351)	$34,990	89
44-45 (convertible S-351)	$43,990	43
40 (coupe SR)	$59,990	7 *
Year Total		139

* Output includes 6 competition models.

1995 Saleen Engines

Code	Engine	Power (hp)	Transmission
4	232-cid (3.8-liter) V-6*	145	M5, A4
E	302-cid (5.0-liter) V-8*	215	M5, A4
N/A	351-cid (5.8-liter) V-8**	371	M5
N/A	351-cid (5.8-liter) V-8 super**	480	M5

* Removed from Saleen S-351s during conversion.
** Actual powertrains used in S-351 production.

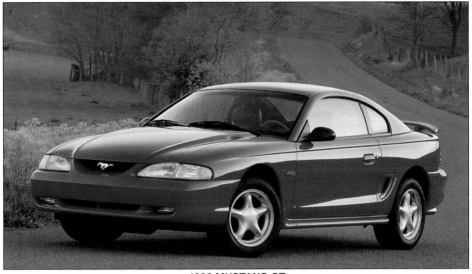

1996 MUSTANG GT

1996 MUSTANG

Cosmetic changes to the Mustang were minimal for 1996. In a nod to the classic design the three-element tail lamps were now oriented vertically, and the combination of clear lenses and complex reflectors was the first such setup on an American car. A new five-spoke, 17-inch wheel became optional on the GT, and the grille received a background screen to conceal the radiator.

The GT received larger stabilizer bars, along with retuned shocks, progressive rate springs, and different bushings. Additional standard equipment on the base model included: AM/FM ETR stereo radio (four speakers); four-wheel power disc brakes; cloth reclining bucket and split folding rear seats; carpeting; console; dual remote mirrors; dual air bags; side glass defoggers; tinted glass; power steering; tilt wheel; oil pressure, tach, temp, and volt gauges; digital clock; trip odometer; front and rear stabilizer bars; front MacPherson struts; visor mirrors; "headlights on" warning tone; intermittent wipers; rocker panel moldings and courtesy lights.

In an effort to keep Mustangs in the hands of the people who paid for them, Ford applied its Passive Anti-Theft System (PATS) to all 1996 GT and Cobra models. PATS-equipped cars cannot be hotwired due to a specially coded ignition key and switch.

1996 Production Chart

Model	Price	Weight	Production
40 (coupe)	$15,180	3,057	61,187
44 (convertible)	$21,060	3,269	15,246
42 (coupe GT)	$17,610	3,279	31,624
45 (convertible GT)	$23,495	3,468	17,917
Year Total			135,620

* Total includes 7,496 SVT Cobra coupes and 2,510 Cobra convertibles.

1996 Engines

Code	Engine	Intake	Power (hp)	Transmission
4	232-cid V-6	EFI	150	M5, A4
W	281-cid V-8 SOHC	EFI	215	M5, A4
V	281-cid V-8 DOHC Cobra	EFI	305	M5

1996 MUSTANG GT 4.6-LITER SOHC V-8

1996 MUSTANG POWERTRAINS

For reasons pertaining to its customer base, federal regulations, and corporate culture, Ford dropped the legendary 5.0-liter V-8 with the 1995 model and debuted the 4.6-liter single-overhead cam (SOHC) "modular" engine in 1996. Measuring 31 cubic inches less than its predecessor (281 vs. 302), the 4.6-liter came to market with the exact same horsepower and torque ratings as the 1995 — 215 and 285, respectively. Although many were skeptical of the new, high-tech engine the overhead camshaft allowed the V-8 to produce its power right up to a 6000 rpm redline, besting the pushrod 5.0 by 1,500 rpms.

The 4.6-liter was part of a family of modular engines Ford developed from a common platform that allowed interchangeability across a line of power plants despite differences in displacement and number of cylinders. Ford engineers assured buyers that the 4.6 liter's unique cylinder head bolt design and spacing meant cylinder and block distortion under stress were no longer factors in a high-performance applica-

tion. Ford's patented oil cooling system, which has no external oil or coolant lines but uses returning water from the radiator, was considered a real contributor to long engine life.

New technologies were incorporated into the modular motor's design, with lightweight pistons and connecting rods and a composite (plastic) intake manifold that increased runner length without taking up as much room as previous alloy versions. The alternator, air-conditioning compressor, and power steering pump were all directly mounted to the block, reducing under hood clutter. Platinum-tipped spark plugs and the accessory drive belt were rated for 100,000 miles before replacement. Partly due to the overhead camshafts, the 4.6 was slightly taller than the 5.0, which meant that accommodations had to be made under the hood.

Ford replaced its Borg-Warner-designed T-5 five-speed manual transmission and four-speed automatic with a beefier T-45 and a 4R70W automatic.

1996 SVT COBRA

1996 SVT COBRA

Ford replaced the Mustang's legendary 5.0-liter pushrod V-8 in 1996 with an engine wearing single overhead camshafts and displacing only 4.6 liters. Although this smooth, efficient "modular" power plant was already in use in the company's Lincoln products, Ford wasn't sure how the rabid Mustang enthusiasts would take to it. The transition was made more attractive when SVT leapfrogged the GT's SOHC setup with a 32-valve, double overhead cam, hand-built version of the new 4.6-liter.

In order to clear the taller DOHC 4.6-liter, a slight dome was built into the Cobra hood and simulated air scoops were installed to distinguish it visually from the GT model. Other appearance changes included "COBRA" lettering stamped into the rear valance panel and a new rear spoiler (the GT-style spoiler became a "customer delete" option this year). A coiled snake emblem appeared at the mouth of the Cobra's grille this year in place of the 1995's galloping pony. Three-inch dual exhaust tips were fitted to the Cobra, an upgrade from the previous year's 2.75-inch units.

Standard equipment included dual airbags, ABS, articulated sport seats (four-way power for the driver), Premium Sound, Power Equipment Group, rear window defroster, air conditioning, cruise control, and remote keyless illuminated entry. The short options list included the Preferred Equipment Package, California emissions components, high-altitude principle-use equipment, and rear spoiler.

Exterior colors offered were Laser Red, Crystal White, Black, and an unusual "Mystic" paint scheme, a combination of colors that showed the green, purple, blue, and black hues in different ways to the light. It was an $815 option for 1996 Cobra coupes chosen by 1,999 customers.

1996 Cobra Production Chart			
Model	**Price**	**Weight**	**Production**
47 (coupe Cobra)	$24,810	3,446	7,496
46 (convertible Cobra)	$27,580	3,620	2,510
Year Total			10,006*

* SVT reports color breakdown as 2,122 Black coupes, 1,053 Black convertibles, 1,999 Mystic coupes, 1,940 Laser Red coupes, 962 Laser Red convertibles, 1,435 Crystal White coupes and 494 Crystal White convertibles.

1996 SVT COBRA 4.6-LITER DOHC V-8

1996 COBRA POWERTRAIN AND SUSPENSION

For its 1996 Cobra, SVT developed an aluminum-block V-8 that produced 305 hp at 5,800 rpm and 300 lbs.-ft. of torque at 4,800 rpm. The block was specially cast by the Teksid company in Italy and shipped to Ford's Romeo, Michigan, engine assembly plant where it was fitted with four-valve heads, twin 57mm throttle bodies, an 80mm Mass Air Sensor and a German-built crankshaft. All 10,000-plus 1996 Cobra motors were built by 12 two-person teams on the special "Niche Line." Conversion from pushrods to double overhead camshafts bumped redlines to 6,800 rpm.

Cobras and GTs shared the new Borg-Warner T-45 five-speed transmission, as these units were deemed capable of handling the torque of the DOHC 4.6-liter. The T-45 design made the transmission casing and bell housing one piece for greater rigidity.

Drivers who submitted the Cobras to extremes of accelerating, braking, and shifting identified a few problem areas. When pushed hard at high ambient temperatures, the 4.6-liter tended to overheat. Ford solved this problem with a cooling upgrade. Many serpentine belt pulleys were replaced with later Cobra pieces when it was determined the originals were prone to making squealing noises or coming off altogether. The new-for-'96 T-45 transmission weakened quickly when subjected to the full force of the Cobra's V-8, with reports of shift forks bending and synchronizer gears wearing excessively.

Enthusiasm for the new DOHC 4.6-liter engine helped to give SVT its highest production run in history, 10,006 of the high-performance Mustang Cobras.

1996 Cobra Engine			
Code	Engine	Power (hp)	Transmission
V	281-cid (4.6-liter) DOHC V-8	305	M5

1996 SALEEN S-281 CONVERTIBLE

1996 SALEEN S-281 AND S-351

In 1996, a member of the Mustang Club of America talked to Steve Saleen at a car show about building an "entry level" model based on Ford's stock 4.6-liter V-8. The "affordable" Saleen, dubbed S-281 after its engine size in cubic inches, featured minimal upgrades to the drive train and interior (which received a new shifter and gauge treatment), but maximum massaging of the suspension and aerodynamics.

Ford's new modular 4.6-liter 281-cid V-8 provided motivation for the Saleen coupes and convertibles. Massive 245/40-18 B.F. Goodrich rubber on 18-inch, five-spoke alloy wheels belied the fact that the S-281 was the lower-priced Saleen. Options included 18-inch magnesium wheels, Recaro seats, a carbon fiber hood, 3.55:1 rear axle, and the convertible-only Speedster package, which featured a hard tonneau cover and a two-point padded rollbar.

Saleen included one-year memberships in both the Mustang Club of America and the Saleen Owners & Enthusiasts Club with the purchase of an S-281. The S-281 became the most popular Saleen model in many years, with 438 examples selling in the first season of production, 30 of which were convertibles sold to the Budget rental car company for use at its premium locations such as Las Vegas.

Twenty S-351s were sold in 1996, and two SRs were built. The SR model was unofficially blended into the S-351 line on which it was based and 1996 S-351s received new Trick Flow heads in place of the previous Edelbrock units.

1996 Saleen Production Chart		
Model	**Price**	**Production**
42 (coupe S-281)	$28,990	193
47 (coupe S-281 Cobra)	$38,900	4
40 (coupe S-351)	$42,990	10
45 (convertible S-281)	$33,500	234*
46 (convertible S-281 Cobra)	$41,000	7
44 (convertible S-351)	$47,990	10
40 (coupe SR)	N/A	2**
Year Total		460

* Production figure includes 30 Budget rental convertibles.
** Output includes 2 competition models.

1996 SALEEN S-281 COBRA

1996 SALEEN S-281 COBRA

In its first year with double overhead camshafts, SVT's Cobra could be taken to the next stage of performance with an S-281 conversion, an option was listed as a separate model or even promoted by Saleen.

Adding the 305-horsepower Cobra option to its lineup was a very smart marketing move for Saleen, because it was a perfect stopgap between the 215-horsepower base S-281 and the fire-breathing 400- and 510-hp S-351. Its aluminum block, four-valve heads, twin 57mm throttle bodies, 80mm mass air sensor, German-built crank and 6,800-rpm redline gave the Cobra 4.6-liter a higher output than any engine Ford installed in a Mustang since 1971. When converted into Saleens, Cobras received all S-281 aerodynamic body pieces plus a composite hood to clear the engine's taller heads and valve covers.

Saleen sold four DOHC S-281 coupes in 1996 and seven convertibles.

1996 Saleen Engines			
Code	Engine	Power (hp)	Transmission
4	232-cid (3.8-liter) V-6*	145	M5, A4
W	281-cid (4.6-liter) V-8 SOHC	215	M5, A4
V	281-cid (4.6-liter) V-8 DOHC Cobra	305	M5
N/A	351-cid (5.8-liter) V-8**	400	M5
N/A	351-cid (5.8-liter) V-8 super**	510	M5

* Removed from Saleen S-351s during conversion.
** Actual powertrains used in S-351 production.

1996-'98 SALEEN BUDGET RENTAL CARS

SALEEN BUDGET RENTAL CARS

With the introduction of the tamer 4.6-liter S-281 came the opportunity to sell Saleen Mustangs to car rental agencies, similar to what Carroll Shelby had done with his GT-350/Hertz program in 1966 and later. Steve Saleen knew the time was right for such an arrangement when the Beverly Hills Rent-A-Car agency bought one of the early 1996 models (and a few others later) for its fleet.

Budget Rent A Car showed the most interest, asking Saleen to submit a prototype and bid for the company's consideration. With approval granted, Budget ordered 30 1996 S-281 convertibles with Ford's leather interior, sport bar and magnesium wheels. Two-thirds of the cars were delivered with automatics and the rest had five-speed manual transmissions. Budget Saleens had their own serial number line, beginning with 96-0001B.

In August of that year, Budget customers on the West Coast (especially at Los Angeles and Las Vegas franchises) started renting the Saleen convertibles for advertised rates of $109 a day with 100 free miles and $.50 for each additional mile. Drivers had to be 25 or older with a clean record and a major credit card with $1,000 available.

The Budget Saleen fleet was equipped with theft-deterrent devices such as Lojack locators, locking lug nuts and steering wheel locks. After serving a year-and-a-half or 26,000 miles the convertibles were refurbished when necessary by Saleen and shipped to wholesalers in Texas and Florida. Console plaques were issued to new owners who provided proof of purchase; the engine compartment identification badges were already in place.

Most of the B-series cars were in good condition when retired, although reports indicate that Budget's maintenance crews were not extremely careful handling the delicate magnesium wheels; many hubs were accidentally reamed out when mounting tires.

Budget ordered 88 Saleen convertibles in 1997 and another 10 in 1998. Total three-year production of B-series Saleens was 128.

SALEEN SPEEDSTER PACKAGE

SALEEN SPEEDSTER PACKAGE

In 1992 Saleen offered a $945 Spyder option on its convertibles that consisted of a rollbar (advertised as a "light bar" for legal reasons) and a soft tonneau cover that protected the Mustang's back seat from the elements. The light bar did not interfere with the stock Mustang power top, and it included a horizontally placed brake lamp. Although only two owners purchased the option in its first year, the simulated two-seater look had appeal and another 22 were ordered for 1993.

The Spyder package carried over to the all-new '94 design, where the light bar was given a softer curve and the fabric tonneau acted as a complete enclosure for the rear seat. In 1996 Saleen took the Spyder concept one step further

by introducing a body-color, hard tonneau as part of the Speedster kit. Shaped to fit snugly against a two-point chassis stiffener (the new name for the rollbar) and front seat headrests, the hard tonneau truly made the Saleen convertible look like a two-seat Speedster. Sliding the large, one-piece plastic shell into place provided a weather resistant area for storing camera equipment, a picnic lunch or other car show paraphernalia. The bad news was the main part of this $2,315 option could not be transported with the convertible top up.

A hanging strap with two seatbelt tabs secured the tonneau cover in place above the back seat.

1997 MUSTANG CONVERTIBLE

1997 MUSTANG

The Mustang was unchanged for 1997, with Ford having pulled off a minor miracle with the 4.6-liter V-8's introduction the year before.

Standard equipment for the base V-6 model included: five-speed manual transmission; PATS anti-theft system; AM/FM ETR stereo radio (four speakers); power front and rear disc brakes; cloth reclining bucket and split folding rear seats; side glass defoggers; tinted glass; power steering; tilt wheel; oil pressure, tach, temp and volt gauges; digital clock; front stabilizer bar; front MacPherson struts; 15-inch steel wheels with covers and P205/65R15 BSW tires;

and rocker panel moldings.

New 17-inch rims with dark gray metallic centers became optional on the GT. A slight change in the upper grille opening allowed more air to the new cooling system.

After a peak in 1995, the new Mustang design had its second straight year of decreased sales at 108,344. For 1997, Ford produced 56,812 base coupes (at a price of $15,880), 11,606 base convertibles ($21,280), 18,464 GT coupes ($18,525), 11,413 GT convertibles ($24,510), 6,961 Cobra coupes ($25,335), and 3,088 Cobra convertibles ($28,135).

1997 Production Chart

Model	Price	Weight	Production
40 (coupe)	$15,880	3,084	56,812
44 (convertible)	$21,280	3,264	11,606
42 (coupe GT)	$18,525	3,288	18,464
45 (convertible GT)	$24,510	3,422	11,413
Year Total			108,344

* Total includes 6,961 SVT Cobra coupes and 3,088 Cobra convertibles.

1997 Engines

Code	Engine	Intake	Power (hp)	Transmission
4	232-cid V-6	EFI	150	M5, A4
W	281-cid V-8 SOHC	EFI	215	M5, A4
V	281-cid V-8 DOHC Cobra	EFI	305	M5

1997 SVT COBRA

1997 SVT COBRA

Cobra coupes and convertibles received slightly larger grille openings in 1997, which they shared with the entire Mustang lineup when Ford re-designed the radiator for better cooling. The grille was also treated to a galloping horse emblem in place of the coiled serpent, but the rear valance panel retained the embossed "Cobra" lettering.

Standard equipment included dual airbags, ABS, articulated sport seats (four-way power for the driver), Premium Sound, Power Equipment Group, rear window defroster, air conditioning, cruise control, front floor mats, dual illuminated visor mirrors and remote keyless illuminated entry. The short options list included the Preferred Equipment Package, California emissions components, high-altitude principle-use equipment and rear spoiler.

For 1997, Pacific Green shared the Cobra paint chip chart with Rio Red, Black, and Crystal White; otherwise, it was business as usual for SVT in 1997, with the company establishing another sales record by an additional 43 units. Of the 10,049 Cobras produced, 6,961 were coupes; 3,088 were convertibles.

1997 Cobra Production Chart

Model	Price	Weight	Production
47 (coupe Cobra)	$25,335	3,446	6,961
46 (convertible Cobra)	$28,135	3,620	3,088
Year Total			10,049*

* SVT reports color breakdown as 2,369 Black coupes, 1,180 Black convertibles, 1,994 Rio Red coupes, 925 Rio Red convertibles, 1,543 Crystal White coupes, 606 Crystal White convertibles, 1,055 Pacific Green coupes and 377 Pacific Green convertibles.

1997 Cobra Engine

Code	Engine	Power (hp)	Transmission
V	281-cid (4.6-liter) DOHC V-8	305	M5

1997 SALEEN S-281

1997 SALEEN S-281 AND S-351

The biggest change for Saleen Mustangs in 1997 was the company's decision to offer its S-351 only in supercharged form. In 1996, 17 of the 20 S-351s it sold had been ordered with the blower. The engine received a boost to its reliability and power through a new high-tech EEC-V management system programmed by Cosworth engineers, select-fit forged aluminum Wiseco pistons with crowns cut to match the combustion chambers and big valves, a spec-ground Competition camshaft, Extrude Honed upper and lower intake manifolds and various 5.0-liter Mustang sensors.

The S-351 also received a standard six-speed Borg-Warner manual transmission, which was mated to a high-performance pressure plate and clutch, balanced driveshaft and a new Torsen differential fitted with 3.27:1 gears.

The company continued production of its successful S-281 with either a 220-hp version

of the 4.6-liter SOHC V-8, or a 310-hp 4.6-liter DOHC (the SVT Cobra's 32-valve engine introduced the previous year). An extra-cost tire upgrade on the S-281 and S-351 were Michelin Pilots measuring 255/40-18 (front) and a super-wide 295/35-18 (rear). All S-351s came standard in 1997 with magnesium wheels.

1997 Saleen Production Chart		
Model	**Price**	**Production**
42 (coupe S-281)	$29,500	113
47 (coupe S-281 Cobra)	$38,900	13
40 (coupe S-351)	$53,500	21
45 (convertible S-281)	$33,990	196*
46 (convertible S-281 Cobra)	$39,500	5
44 (convertible S-351)	$57,990	19
40 (coupe SR)	N/A	5**
Year Total		372

* Production figure includes 88 Budget rental convertibles.
** Figure includes 2 competition models.

1997 S-351 SPEEDSTER PRESS CAR

SALEEN PRESS CARS

Every car company, no matter how big or small, must retain a number of sample vehicles each year to be used by media, potential fleet customers and various other folks who need to be impressed. Ford Motor Company, for example, has hundreds of cars, trucks and SUVs available at any time around the world for members of the press to evaluate and for display at special events such as golf tournaments and NASCAR races.

Saleen Autosport's first press car was 84-0032, the white hatchback Steve Saleen built as a prototype for the entire series. Several members of the car hobby press drove it and promoted it as an attractive alternative to Ford's own SVO Mustang. Its existence also convinced some Ford dealers to order copies from Saleen, after which it was used for photography more than for evaluation.

Some Saleen press cars remained entirely stock while in the company's hands. Others were upgraded to reflect model year changes. For example, 88-0002, a white convertible, was built in February of 1988 and retained by Saleen for press use. It was updated to 1989 specs in September with a new graphics package and five-spoke wheels.

Perhaps the most overworked of the Saleen press vehicles was 87-0001, a white hatchback driven by every media hotfoot in the business before it was "retired" to Michigan to serve as the engineering mule and EPA test car for the SSC's 300-hp 5.0-liter powertrain.

Because these press vehicles have colorful histories and enough published photos to fill a scrapbook, they are sought after by collectors. In the Saleen world, just about any Mustang with the serial number 0001 was likely used by the company for promotion, but several cars were pulled from the production line toward the middle or end of their seasons to serve as press vehicles as well.

1998 MUSTANG GT

1998 MUSTANG

There were not many changes to the Mustang line in 1998, the final year before the car received a mild facelift. Base, GT, and Cobra in coupe and convertible body styles again comprised the Mustang lineup. The 3.8-liter V-6 (base Mustangs) and 4.6-liter V-8 (GT and Cobra models) were again the engines used, with the GT's power plant, gaining 10 hp from 215 to 225 hp.

Ford introduced two new option packages: a GT Sport Group that included the 17-inch aluminum wheels; hood and wraparound fender stripes; engine oil cooler; and the V-6 Sport Appearance Group that gave the buyer 16-inch cast-aluminum wheels, rear spoiler, leather-wrapped steering wheel, and a lower body side accent stripe.

Improvements included polished aluminum wheels and a premium sound system with cassette and CD capability added as standard equipment on the base coupe and convertible. Ford's SecuriLock anti-theft system was standard on the Mustang.

1998 produced a big spike in Mustang production, with 175,522 going to new homes.

1998 Production Chart			
Model	**Price**	**Weight**	**Production**
40 (coupe)	$15,970	3,065	99,801
44 (convertible)	$20,470	3,210	21,254
42 (coupe GT)	$19,970	3,227	28,789
45 (convertible GT)	$23,970	3,400	17,024
Year Total			175,522
* Total includes 5,174 SVT Cobra coupes and 3,480 Cobra convertibles.			

1998 Engines				
Code	**Engine**	**Intake**	**Power (hp)**	**Transmission**
4	232-cid V-6	EFI	150	M5, A4
W	281-cid V-8 SOHC	EFI	215	M5, A4
V	281-cid V-8 DOHC Cobra	EFI	305	M5

1998 SVT COBRA

1998 SVT COBRA

1998 was another year without substantial change for the Cobra, the most noticeable being a switch to five-spoke wheels similar to what SVT put on the 1995 R models. The Cobra's firewall-to-tower triangulated brace disappeared again in 1998, and the grille featured a stock Mustang's running horse emblem. The rear valance panel read "Cobra."

Interior changes mirrored those on the stock GT Mustang. The console was re-designed; the clock pod was removed from the instrument panel, leaving the radio in charge of telling time and a CD player became standard with the premium sound system. The console-mounted ashtray was replaced with cup holders.

At some point in the model year, Tremec began building the Cobra's T-45 transmission under license from Borg-Warner. Tremec's changes strengthened the five-speed and ended customer complaints about bent shift forks and ruined synchronizer gears.

Standard equipment included dual airbags, ABS, articulated sport seats (four-way power for the driver), Premium Sound, and Power Equipment Group. The short options list included the Electronic Leather/Trim Group, California emissions components, high-altitude principle-use equipment, and rear spoiler.

1998 Cobra Production Chart

Model	Price	Weight	Production
47 (coupe Cobra)	$25,710	3,446	5,174
46 (convertible Cobra)	$28,510	3,620	3,480
Year Total			8,654*

* SVT reports color breakdown as 1,708 Black coupes, 1,256 Black convertibles, 1,236 Laser Red coupes, 842 Laser Red convertibles, 958 Crystal White coupes, 578 Crystal White convertibles, 563 Atlantic Blue coupes, 249 Atlantic Blue convertibles, 709 Canary Yellow coupes and 555 Canary Yellow convertibles.

1998 Cobra Engine

Code	Engine	Power (hp)	Transmission
W	281-cid (4.6-liter) DOHC V-8	305	M5

1998 SALEEN S-351

1998 SALEEN S-281 AND S-351

Saleen S-281 sales slowed down for 1998 to 183 units, partly due to the inadequate performance of the 4.6-liter engine. Ford's 10 additional horsepower was not enough to spark greater interest among the enthusiast public, and Saleen was reluctant to spend company resources modifying a power plant that would be receiving a substantial grunt upgrade from the factory the following year. Instead, the engine only received Saleen's high-performance spark plug wires, a high-flow air filter and Borla mufflers.

Casinos purchased a total of five '98 Saleen S-281 Mustangs to promote as jackpot giveaway prizes.

The $56,990 price tag on the super-fast S-351 was likely the cause of that model's drop to 22 sales for the year. Pricing also affected the race-inspired SR version, of which only three

were built. Due to a clever marketing program, Saleen had no problem selling all 10 of its yellow-black-and-white SA-15 anniversary supercharged convertibles.

1998 Saleen Production Chart

Model	Price	Production
42 (coupe S-281)	$26,990	57
47 (coupe S-281 Cobra)	$36,990	14
40 (coupe S-351)	$56,990	10
45 (convertible S-281)	$32,990	81*
46 (convertible S-281 Cobra)	$39,590	21
44 (convertible S-351)	$60,990	12
45 (convertible SA-15)	$42,500	10
40 (coupe SR)	$125,000	3**
Year Total		208

* Production figure includes 10 Budget rental convertibles.
** Figure includes 3 competition models.

1998 SALEEN SA-15

1998 SALEEN SA-15

To commemorate the company's 15th year in business, Saleen Inc. released a limited series of 10 Bright Yellow S-281 Speedsters with black markings, composite hoods and special supercharged 4.6-liter engines. As Saleen tradition dictated, the cars were built after production of the regular lines had ceased for the year. All show shipping dates in December except for one that was finished on Jan. 15.

Buyers were encouraged to raid the Saleen parts department in order to personalize their SA-15s in addition to the base model's MSRP of $42,500. As a result, no two were built alike other than body and wheel color and power plant. Seven shipped with the 10-inch rear wheel upgrade; eight had 13-inch front brakes; six were ordered with the 3.55:1 rear axle gears; and six had Saleen leather. There was one automatic transmission in the bunch.

The SA-15 was truly a special edition, as it was the first 4.6-liter model Saleen marketed with a supercharger, although it was technically not a "factory-installed" piece of equipment, but modified by the parts department.

1999 MUSTANG GT COUPE

1999 MUSTANG

Not content to merely spruce up a six-year-old design, Ford's stylists gave the 1999 Mustang line a much-appreciated facelift and tummy tuck, while prescribing some steroid therapy. The smooth, mostly feminine, curves of the 1994 through 1998 Mustang were replaced with strong creases and straight lines. The sides of the car took on a more vertical angle, and the tallest scoop ever to grace a Mustang was installed just behind the door. This "pumping up" of the previous design reminded many Mustang fans of the changes that had given the original 1965 a body-builder look in 1967.

On GT models, the hood grew a simulated recessed scoop that recalled the air-grabber the 1968 sported when it received its first 428-cid V-8. GT exhaust tips also were enlarged slightly, from 2.75 inches to 3 inches. Up front, the Mustang's headlights took on a sinister appearance. Taillights received the same treatment as the rest of the car, going from soft and rounded

to hard and harsh. Looking for ways to reduce weight at every turn, designers created a new deck lid made from a sheet-molded compound.

While the exterior improvements were enough to bring new customers, there were refinements in areas that couldn't be seen so easily, such as the revised floor pan sealing and foam-packed rocker panels— both of which reduced road noise. Engineers reduced a troublesome "mid-car shake" on the convertible models through the use of sub-frame connectors and gained a tiny bit of rear suspension travel on all models by raising the drive tunnel 1.5 inches.

As the Mustang drew nearer to the end of the century, it received new technology in the form of an all-speed Traction Control System (TCS), a $230 option that worked in harmony with the also-optional (on base models) ABS to reduce tire spin in slippery conditions. Taller "Mustangers" no doubt appreciated the extra inch of travel built into the driver's seat for 1999.

1999 MUSTANG 260-HORSEPOWER 4.6-LITER SOHC V-8

260-HORSEPOWER 4.6-LITER V-8 ENGINE

The biggest boost to the Mustang's reputation for 1999 was an increase in the 4.6-liter V-8's output from 225 horsepower to 260. Ford engineers were able to squeeze more juice from its sturdy single overhead camshaft power plant by replacing the 1996 through 1998 heads with a "performance improvement" (PI) design that increased flow through larger intake ports.

In addition, new camshafts were installed for higher and longer lift, intake manifold runners were lengthened to give a straighter path for the incoming air/fuel mixture, and larger intake valves were used.

The modifications not only increased the 4.6-liter's horsepower, but improved its breathing efficiency in the middle to high range.

A Tremec-built T45 five-speed manual transmission and 3.27:1 rear axle gears were standard on the GT model.

1999 Production Chart			
Model	**Price**	**Weight**	**Production**
40 (coupe)	$16,470	3,069	73,180
44 (convertible)	$21,070	3,211	19,299
42 (coupe GT)	$20,870	3,273	19,634
45 (convertible GT)	$24,870	3,429	13,699
Year Total			133,637
* Total includes 4,040 SVT Cobra coupes and 4,055 Cobra convertibles.			

1999 Engines				
Code	**Engine**	**Intake**	**Power (hp)**	**Transmission**
4	232-cid V-6	EFI	190	M5, A4
X	281-cid V-8 SOHC	EFI	260	M5, A4
V	281-cid V-8 DOHC Cobra	EFI	320	M5

1999 MUSTANG 190-HORSEPOWER 3.8-LITER V-6

190-HORSEPOWER 3.8-LITER V-6 ENGINE

Ford raised the level of its base Mustang performance for 1999, bringing its power-to-weight ratio in line with sporty coupes offered by the competition.

The default power plant was Ford's 3.8-liter (232-cid) "Essex" V-6, which gained a substantial 40 horsepower that year for a total of 190. Aiding this transformation was a new dual-runner intake manifold for increased airflow and slick piston coatings that reduced internal friction. Although the V-6 did not benefit from the V-8's overhead camshaft technology, it did receive a balance shaft to counteract vibrations inherent in the earlier version of the engine.

Base V-6 Mustangs came standard with a five-speed manual transmission, and the four-speed automatic was an extra-cost option.

1999 MUSTANG GT 17-INCH WHEEL

1999 MUSTANG GT WHEELS/TIRES/ BRAKES

The Mustang GT got a new wheel design in 1999—a 17-incher with five narrow spokes centered by an unobtrusive plastic cap. Wrapped around the fresh silver rims were P245/45ZR17 Goodyear Eagle ZR high-performance blackwall radial tires.

Buyers of 1994 through 1998 Mustang GTs had complained about the car's "tucked in" rear wheels—the product of a narrow axle specified more for engineering reasons than aesthetic value—that subtracted from its muscle car stance. That problem was addressed in 1999 by increasing the GT's track by 1.4 inches, a move that improved its handling and appearance all at the same time.

Four-wheel disc brakes were standard equipment on the GT, just as they had been since introduced in 1994, but the 1999 system featured twin-piston aluminum calipers and other high-tech components that reduced the Mustang's unsprung weight by a total of 10 pounds.

Other suspension improvements for '99 included new linear-rate springs, revalved shock absorbers and a retuned stabilizer bar, changes that made the ride quality better and decreased the GT's turning circle by three feet.

1999 MUSTANG 35TH ANNIVERSARY LIMITED EDITION

1999 MUSTANG 35TH ANNIVERSARY MODEL

To commemorate the Mustang's 35th anniversary in grand style, Ford produced a small run (5,000 were announced) of Limited Edition models that stickered for $2,695 above the cost of a GT.

Features included a special, raised hood scoop (at the end of a wide black stripe); rear deck wing; stand-out side scoops, black honeycomb deck lid appliqué; body-color rocker moldings; Midnight Black GT leather interior with silver leather inserts; special floor mats with 35th anniversary script; and special aluminum shift knob (five-speeds only). Exterior colors were limited to Black, Silver, Crystal White and Performance Red. "Mustangers" did not realize it at the time, but the Limited Edition incorporated many of the cosmetic upgrades that would become standard with the 2001 model.

Of the 4,628 Limited Editions produced in 1999, 2,318 were coupes and 2,310 were built as convertibles.

1999 SVT COBRA

1999 SVT COBRA

The Mustang V-6 and GT models received major facelifts and several chassis and engine improvements for their 35th anniversary year. Taking the platform one step further, SVT took the new car and built one of the most awesome Ford muscle cars of the 20th Century by adding 15 horsepower to the already potent 4.6-liter DOHC V-8.

Cobra changes reflected the standard Mustang's new starchier design, but left out the running horse's chrome surround and installed the traditional coiled serpent emblem in place of the stock car's 35th Anniversary logo. An SVT-designed front bumper cover and scoopless hood managed to round off the 1999 Mustang's harsh edges.

SVT debuted a new 17-inch five-spoke, star-shaped wheel on the 1999 Cobra that offered a nearly unobstructed view of the large disc brakes at each corner. Brake sizes and specs were unchanged for 1999, but Brembo became the supplier. Standard equipment included dual airbags, ABS, articulated sport seats (four-way

power for the driver), Premium Sound, Power Equipment Group, rear window defroster, air conditioning, cruise control, front floor mats, dual illuminated visor mirrors, and remote keyless illuminated entry. The short options list included the rear spoiler and a smoker's package. Four exterior colors were offered: Ultra White, Ebony, Rio Red, and Electric Green. New upholstery patterns and colors were available, although only in leather as there were no cloth options for seats in 1999.

An unusual balance was reached for 1999, with coupe and convertible sales nearly equal. Of the 8,095 total cars sold, 4,040 were coupes; 4,055 were the convertibles.

1999 Cobra Production Chart			
Model	**Price**	**Weight**	**Production**
47 (coupe Cobra)	$27,470	3,430	4,040
46 (convertible Cobra)	$31,470	3,560	4,055
Year Total			8,095*

* SVT reports color breakdown as 1,619 Black coupes, 1,755 Black convertibles, 1,292 Laser Red coupes, 1,251 Laser Red convertibles, 794 Ultra White coupes, 731 Ultra White convertibles, 408 Electric Green coupes and 318 Electric Green convertibles.

1999 SVT COBRA 4.6-LITER DOHC 320-HORSEPOWER V-8

320-HP DOHC V-8

The Cobra's 4.6-liter DOHC engine was given a different combustion chamber design and reconfigured intake port geometry that created a more efficient mixing of the air/fuel mixture. Improved combustion raised the Cobra V-8 to a factory-claimed 320 hp and 317 lbs.-ft. of torque. A coil-on-plug ignition system and new type of knock sensor contributed to the Cobra's reliability and smooth power delivery.

Handling all that power was the Borg-Warner-designed T-45 five-speed introduced on the 1996 Mustang and Cobra models, but for 1999 the Cobra unit was built by Tremec. These units can be identified as being different from the Borg-Warner-built transmissions by the "Tremec" name stamped into the housing.

Cobra's reputation for high-performance continued to grow in its seventh year of production, but with one glitch. Car magazines, while testing the 1999 4.6-liter, reported that their test cars seemed slower than the 1998 models. Consideration was given to the extra weight of the IRS system, but in the end, dynamometer tests revealed the new Cobra was not reaching its advertised output. In a rare move, Ford ceased the sale of unsold Cobras at dealerships on Aug. 6, 1999, and recalled those models already in private hands. SVT replaced the intake manifold, engine management computer and entire exhaust system from the catalytic converter back on every single 1999 produced. An "Authorized Modifications" label was placed at the front of the engine compartment as each car was fixed. SVT's efforts impressed the media as well as its customers.

1999 Cobra Engine			
Code	**Engine**	**Power (hp)**	**Transmission**
V	281-cid (4.6-liter) DOHC V-8	320	M5

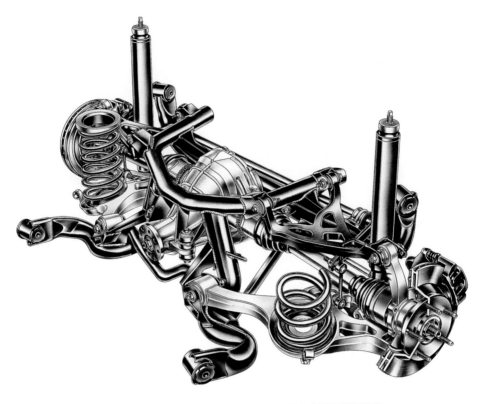

1999 SVT COBRA INDEPENDENT REAR SUSPENSION

COBRA INDEPENDENT REAR SUSPENSION (IRS)

SVT's 35th anniversary gift to the Mustang world was a long-awaited independent rear suspension (IRS) using short and long arms mounted on a tubular subframe. With an eye toward Mustang GT owners who would want the same IRS system on their cars, SVT designed it to mount to the same four points as the stock solid rear axle. Although the IRS weighed 80 pounds more than the straight axle, it reduced the all-important unsprung weight by 125 pounds, resulting in sharper handling and a better ride. SVT applied much stiffer rear springs—470 lbs./in. versus 210 on the solid-axle GT—and a thicker sway bar than ever before at 26mm. Front springs were more traditional 500-lbs./in. units working in concert with a 28mm stabilizer bar.

The rear axle's differential case was made of aluminum, although the same gears as before were installed. The Mustang's optional all-speed Traction Control System (TCS) was standard on the Cobra, providing a great safety benefit as it worked with the car's ABS to limit wheelspin in slippery conditions.

1999 SALEEN S-281 CONVERTIBLE

1999 SALEEN S-281

A number of factors made 1999 a bumper sales year for Saleen, the first of which was a set of new performance improvement ("PI") heads for the 4.6-liter SOHC engine that boosted stock Mustang GT output to 260 horsepower. Saleen engineers added lower-diameter accessory pulleys, a performance air filter, less-restrictive mufflers, freer-flowing exhaust pipes and a computer with a taste for premium unleaded to achieve 285 emissions-legal horsepower.

Saleen had spent some time with the EPA leading up to the 1999 season, the result being a certified factory supercharger option for the S-281 that produced 350 horsepower. Tremec's five-speed manual transmission was stock on both versions of the S-281.

The Racecraft suspension followed the standard Saleen formula, with a switch to P255/35ZR18 Pirelli P7000 tires on all-new 18 x 9-inch wheels in front and P265/35ZR18 Pirellis in back. Magnesium wheels were no longer available, but chrome-finished aluminum rims could be ordered for $935. Brakes were the standard GT's 10.8-inch front and 10.5-inch rear discs, and there was a 13-inch brake option.

Seats were stock Mustang GT units, but the $2,989 upgrade to Saleen leather-covered sport models was a popular choice.

The new-for-'99 S-281 and Speedster were unveiled alongside their S-351 stablemate in January during a press party at Irvine's Planet Hollywood. The three cars displayed were early development vehicles; S-281 production did not get under way for the year until February.

1999 Saleen Production Chart		
Model	Price	Production
42 (coupe S-281)	$27,990	183
47 (coupe S-281 Cobra)	$37,695	8
40 (coupe S-351)	$49,990	20
45 (convertible S-281)	$31,790	170
46 (convertible S-281 Cobra)	$41,595	12
44 (convertible S-351)	$54,490	26
40 (coupe SR)	N/A	2*
Year Total		421
* Figure includes 1 competition model.		

1999 SALEEN S-351

1999 SALEEN S-351

Late in 1998 Saleen Inc. published the following information in its *Confidential Certified Dealer Information and Ordering Guide*:

"Saleen will continue to build the S-351 through Dec. 31, 1999. Regardless of whether an S-351 is built from a 1999 or 2000 model year chassis it will be designated in the Saleen Owners Registry as a 1999 model. The last ship date for the 1999 S-351 will be no later than Dec. 31, 1999. Saleen reserves the right to stop accepting orders past any date in which this deadline cannot be met. Saleen plans to announce a new model designed to replace the world famous S-351 in the very near future."

The antiquated architecture of the S-351's pushrod engine was making it harder to bring in line with EPA and CARB regulations. The company had three options for future S-351s: commit the money and resources to developing a new strategy for an engine Ford was phasing out; stop selling them in California; or end the line with 1999. Saleen had already received three years' worth of provisions from the EPA in order to produce the S-351, so '99 would be its final season.

Tailpipe output was not really the SVT Lightning-based V-8's biggest problem. It was in the area of evaporative emissions—in layman's terms, gas tank fumes—where the S-351 could not so easily be brought into compliance. Unlike the S-281 and GT, the S-351 had never been converted to a "returnless" fuel delivery system. Its constant loop carried premium unleaded from the stock Mustang gas tank to the engine, with the unused portion returned by separate line to the tank. Along the way, the fuel picked up heat, which caused the gas in the tank to expand and give off more fumes into the atmosphere.

In order to meet EVAP standards Saleen engineers devised a clever, but complicated, method for cooling the gas tank with small fans blowing air through tubes and around a special shroud. The tubes were directed through the trunk, right behind the back seat.

1999 SALEEN SUPERCHARGED 4.6-LITER SOHC V-8

SALEEN SUPER-CHARGED 4.6-LITER

Building its own in-house certification lab meant Saleen Inc. was in a position in 1999 to develop many power-enhancing products for Ford's 4.6-liter SOHC V-8, its first offering being a "Series I" Eaton supercharger option for $3,995 which turned the S-281 into a 350-horsepower beast.

Eager to show the new blown motor to the aftermarket industry, Saleen engineers developed an initial pre-production prototype in time for the November 1998 SEMA show in Las Vegas. The compressor was identical to the unit installed on the 10 Saleen SA-15s. The intake manifold was different to match Ford's new PI head ports. Although it looked road-ready at SEMA, the supercharged 4.6 would not enter production until April, after passing its 50-state certification.

Superchargers proved very popular with the S-281 buyers, who snatched up 122 of the factory-installed Eaton blowers as individual options or as part of the $6,440 R-code package

that included a brake upgrade. For model year 2000 and later, all S-281s ordered with the Series I supercharger were given the designation S/C, although they were not technically considered to be different models. In 2001, the Series II blower added an integral boost bypass valve. A Series III design was never put into production after development and evaluation.

1999 Saleen Engines			
Code	Engine	Power (hp)	Transmission
4	232-cid (3.8-liter) V-6*	190	M5, A4
X	281-cid (4.6-liter) V-8 SOHC	285	M5, A4
X	281-cid (4.6-liter) V-8 SOHC super	350	M5, A4
V	281-cid (4.6-liter) V-8 DOHC Cobra	320	M5
N/A	351-cid (5.8-liter) V-8 super**	495	M6

* Removed from Saleen S-351s during conversion.
** Actual powertrain used in S-351 production.

2000 MUSTANG

2000 MUSTANG

Three new colors, Sunburst Gold, Performance Red, and Amazon Gold, replaced Chrome Yellow, Rio Red, and Dark Green Satin. That was about it for the obvious changes to the 2000 Mustang.

Two new safety features were added. Child seat tether anchor brackets were attached to the rear seating areas of all Mustangs. An interior deck lid release with glow-in-the-dark illumination became standard equipment after news reports of carjacking victims being locked in the trucks of their cars.

The base coupe listed for $16,520; the base convertible, $21,370; the GT coupe, $21,015; and the GT convertible, $25,270.

2000 Production Chart			
Model	**Price**	**Weight**	**Production**
40 (coupe)	$16,520	3,064	121,026
44 (convertible)	$21,370	3,203	41,368
42 (coupe GT)	$21,015	3,227	32,321
45 (convertible GT)	$25,270	3,375	20,224
Year Total			215,693 *
* Includes 300 SVT Cobra R coupes			

2000 Engines				
Code	**Engine**	**Intake**	**Power (hp)**	**Transmission**
4	232-cid V-6	EFI	190	M5, A4
X	281-cid V-8 SOHC	EFI	260	M5, A4
H	330-cid V-8 DOHC Cobra R	EFI	385	M6

2000 SVT COBRA R

2000 SVT COBRA R

SVT cancelled production of street-model 2000 Cobras to fix all of the recalled 1999 cars and to build the most powerful, brutal Mustang since the Boss 429 — the 2000 Cobra R. The engineers at SVT developed an all-new power plant for the 2000 R, a cast-iron 5.4-liter DOHC, 32-valve V-8 and tweaked until it turned out an awe-inspiring 385 hp and 385 lbs.-ft. of torque.

The R driver's only points of contact were competition-quality components: Racing Recaro seats, a thickly padded steering wheel and a B&M Ripper shifter. Certain stock Cobra pieces were left off of the R to reduce weight, including some soundproofing material, trunk trim, spare tire cover, rear seat, air-conditioning and power seats. The standard equipment list included dual airbags, independent rear suspension, ABS, a 20-gallon Fuel Safe bladder-type fuel cell, full-size spare tire, front air splitter, seven-inch rear wing, power dome hood, SecuriLock passive anti-theft system, Recaro seats,

180-mph speedometer, B&M Ripper shifter with leather-wrapped shift knob, Power Equipment Group (including dual electric remote-control mirrors, power side windows, power door locks and power deck lid release).

When tested, the 3,590-lb. R zipped to 60 mph in less than five seconds, with a top speed of more than 170. Speeds at redline for each gear were astounding for a Mustang — 47 mph in first; 68 in second; 98 in third; 141 in fourth; 170-plus in fifth; and 160-plus in sixth.

At $54,995, the SVT Mustang Cobra R models sold all 300 units before the first cars hit dealer showrooms.

2000 Cobra Production Chart

Model	Price	Weight	Production
47 (coupe Cobra R)	$54,995	3,590	300
Year Total			300*
*All 300 Cobra Rs were painted Performance Red with Dark Charcoal interiors.			

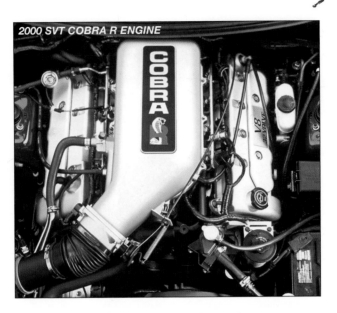

2000 SVT COBRA R ENGINE

2000 SVT COBRA R POWERTRAIN AND SUSPENSION

Digging into the modular family parts bin, SVT engineers developed an all-new power plant for the 2000 R: a cast-iron 5.4-liter DOHC, 32-valve V-8 tweaked to 385 hp. The 5.4-liter's cylinder bore is identical to that of the 4.6-liter engine found in the street Cobra, but stroke is 15.8mm longer, which provides the greater displacement.

Fresh air was fed into the V-8 through a K&N cylindrical air filter, single oval-bore throttle body and 80mm Mass Air Sensor. A lot of aluminum four-valve head work went into the creation of all that power; peak airflow was increased by 25 percent over standard Cobra components. T56 six-speed manual transmission — the first six-speed ever installed in a factory-built Mustang — was specified to handle the 5.4-liter's tremendous torque. An aluminum driveshaft led to the 8.8-inch aluminum-case differential. Induction-hardened GKN half shafts are the final link

to the rear wheels. Final drive ratio was a short 3.55:1 for increased acceleration.

Eibach coil springs lowered the car 1.5 inches in front and 1.0 at the rear and made the chassis 30 to 40 percent stiffer than the 1999 Cobra. Brembo four-wheel disc brakes were activated through four-piston aluminum calipers. Air inlets designed into the Cobra fog light openings were used to provide extra brake cooling.

Five-spoke, 18-inch wheels were fitted with 265/40ZR-18 B. F. Goodrich g-Force tires, which contributed somewhat to the R's astounding 1.0g of lateral acceleration.

2000 Cobra R Engine			
Code	Engine	Power (hp)	Transmission
H	330-cid (5.4-liter) DOHC V-8	385	M6

2000 SALEEN S-281

2000 SALEEN S-281

Saleen Inc. nearly tripled its sales figures for its Mustang-based S-281 coupes and convertibles in the year 2000, with 974 examples going to new homes. Adding to the good news was the high percentage of buyers loading up their Saleens with expensive optional equipment such as chromed wheels, 3.55:1 rear axle gears, Speedster packages and leather-covered Recaro seats.

The S-281 gained 65 horsepower and an "S/C" suffix when ordered with the Series I blower. Gone was the R-code supercharger options package. Instead, the S/C was given its own pricing system but the company did not consider it to be a separate model. The supercharger package included all S-281 standard equipment plus the twin-gauge pod (displaying boost and intercooler temperature). Sales of the S/C accounted for 45 percent of S-281 sales for the year, with 435 orders for superchargers.

The base S-281 engine was still rated at 285 horsepower (25 more than Ford's Mustang GT) due to a modified EEC-V strategy, underdrive pulleys, performance air filter, less-restrictive mufflers and freer-flowing exhaust pipes. The Tremec five-speed was stock, with Ford's four-speed automatic available at extra cost and both transmissions working through a standard 3.27:1 rear axle.

The S-281 Racecraft suspension had a few minor changes for 2000, including slightly taller springs and a switch from Carrera to Bilstein as manufacturer of its shock absorbers and struts. Standard wheels and tires were P255/35ZR18 Pirelli P7000s on 18 x 9-inch wheels in front and P265/35ZR18 Pirellis in back. An upgrade package brought Pirelli's PZeros.

2000 Saleen Production Chart		
Model	**Price**	**Production**
42 (coupe S-281)	$29,990	307
42 (coupe S-281 S/C)	$35,460	232
45 (convertible S-281)	$33,900	232
42 (convertible S-281 S/C)	$39,460	203
42 (coupe SR)	N/A	5*
Year Total		979
* Figure includes 5 competition models.		

2001 MUSTANG GT CONVERTIBLE

2001 MUSTANG

Ford reduced the number of Mustang feature combinations from the previous year's 2,600 to approximately 50 for 2001. Standard, Deluxe, and Premium Equipment Groups became the only offered option packages.

For the base coupe, the Standard Equipment Group included 15-inch painted alloy wheels; P205/65R15 all-season tires; electronic ignition; multi-port fuel injection; four-wheel disc brakes; stereo CD/radio/cassette; air conditioning; driver and passenger airbag; split fold-down rear seat; and SecuriLock Passive Anti-Theft System.

Base or GT model Deluxe Equipment Group included a rear spoiler; power driver's seat; leather-wrapped steering wheel (GT only); cloth front sport bucket seats (GT coupe/convertible); speed control and 17-inch painted aluminum wheels (GT only). These options could be added to the Deluxe package: automatic transmission; anti-lock brake system with Traction Control (requires automatic on coupe; standard on GT);

Sport Appearance Group (V-6 only); Mach 460 in-dash six-disc CD changer and AM/FM radio; leather-trimmed front bucket seats (V-6 convertible only); and leather-trimmed front Sport bucket seats (GT convertible only).

Ordering the Premium Equipment Group gave the Mustang buyer an automatic transmission (optional on convertibles); 16-inch bright alloy wheels; P225/55R-16 all-season tires; Mach 460 in-dash six-disc CD changer and AM/FM radio; leather-wrapped steering wheel; anti-lock brake system with Traction Control; leather-trimmed front sport bucket seats (GT only); and 17-inch five-spoke premium alloy wheels (GT only). Leather-trimmed front bucket seats, standard on convertibles, could also be added optionally.

All models came standard with a rear window defroster, while the "smoker's package" and block heater became dealer-installed accessories. A new six-disc CD changer became optional with the Mach 460 sound system.

2001 MUSTANG GT BULLITT

2001 BULLITT

In 1968 Mustang fans saw their car rise to icon status when Steve McQueen drove a green fastback through the hills of San Francisco. The movie Bullitt featured the most realistic chase scene ever shot, with McQueen's Frank Bullitt chasing bad guys in a '68 Dodge Charger.

In 2001 Ford Motor Company paid homage to the Bullitt legend with a limited production special model based on its popular Mustang GT platform. The coupe-only model featured exterior enhancements that visually and emotionally connected it to the famous chase scene. Unique to the Bullitt Mustang were special side scoops, 17-inch American Racing aluminum wheels, a lowered suspension, modified C-pillars, and quarter panel molding that set the car apart from a stock GT. Rocker panel moldings enhanced the lowered appearance. A bold, brushed aluminum fuel filler door was prominently placed on the quarter panel. Special Bullitt badging and polished-rolled tailpipe tips further distin-

guished the car.

Providing 270 hp was a mildly modified 4.6-liter, with a twin 57mm-bore throttle body, cast aluminum intake manifold, and high-flow mufflers.

The Bullitt package listed for $3,695 above the cost of a GT for 2001.

2001 Production Chart

Model	Price	Weight	Production
40 (coupe)	$16,995	3,064	*
40 (deluxe coupe)	$17,560	3,066	*
44 (deluxe convertible)	$22,410	3,208	*
40 (premium coupe)	$18,790	3,066	*
44 (premium convertible)	$24,975	3,208	*
42 (deluxe coupe GT)	$22,630	3,241	*
45 (deluxe convertible GT)	$26,885	3,379	*
42 (premium coupe GT)	$23,780	3,241	*
45 (premium convertible GT)	$28,035	3,379	*
42 (Bullitt coupe)	$26,320	3,241	5,582
Year Total			155,161 *

2001 GT HOOD SCOOP

MUSTANG RETRO STYLING

For years automakers could not move far enough away from the styling cues of the 1960s. Square, blocky, muscular designs were being replaced by jelly bean shapes that pleased the wind tunnel technicians more than consumers.

When Dodge brought its Viper roadster — a design that owed much to Carroll Shelby's awesome Cobras—to market, its acceptance by the public was a green flag for all manufacturers to dust off some old styling cues and embrace the past.

Ford's 1994 Mustang wore certain "retro" elements such as three-lens taillamps, running horse emblem and side scoop. Overall, the car broke with tradition by being too aerodynamic, too slippery. The company's desire to give America a new Mustang that recalled the enormously successful original model was apparent in 1999 when the model received some surgery that squared the shoulders and pumped up the body. A 2001 touch-up brought a more aggres-sive, 1960s-style appearance to the GT by adding a fake hood scoop and kicked-up rear wing.

Ford took the public's desire for a retro Mustang seriously in 2005 by designing a body that was part Boss 302, part 1966 Shelby and part 1970 fastback. The GT wheels, three-spoke steering wheel, chromed bezels and pleated seat vinyl look as if they were found in a time capsule at the American Racing plant, and the interior—with its three-spoke steering wheel, chromed bezels and pleated seat vinyl—make it feel like the Mach 1 never went out of production.

2001 Engines				
Code	Engine	Intake	Power (hp)	Transmission
4	232-cid V-6	EFI	190	M5, A4
X	281-cid V-8 SOHC	EFI	260	M5, A4
X	281-cid V-8 SOHC Bullitt	EFI	270	M5
H	330-cid V-8 DOHC Cobra	EFI	320	M5

GT 'BULLITT' WHEEL

One of the most popular aftermarket wheels for muscle cars in the 1960s was the Torq-Thrust design from American Racing. A simple five-spoke pattern forged out of aluminum, the wheel's center was usually painted charcoal or black while the rim itself remained its natural metallic color.

The Torq-Thrust became an icon of Mustang performance with its appearance on Steve McQueen's 1968 fastback in the movie Bullitt, which naturally led Ford to consider installing an updated version on its 2001 commemorative coupes named for the action film. Knowing there would be a high demand for the retro rims, Ford made the Bullitt wheels available as part of a GT premium package that also included leather seats and the Mach 460 stereo with six-disc in-dash CD changer.

Tires were identical whether the standard or premium GT model was ordered: P245/45ZR17 Goodyears.

2001 SVT COBRA

2001 SVT COBRA

After fixing its 1999 model to produce the 320 horsepower SVT had promised, the formula was mostly unchanged for 2001. Minor exterior changes included the return of "Cobra" lettering imprinted into the rear fascia and five new colors (True Blue, Zinc Yellow, Mineral Gray, Performance Red and Laser Red) for a total palette of eight.

Standard equipment included dual airbags, ABS, Traction Control System, articulated sport seats (a new-for-2001 design with four-way power for the driver), Premium Sound (with a six-disc in-dash CD player), Power Equipment Group, rear window defroster, air conditioning, cruise control, front floor mats, dual illuminated visor mirrors and remote keyless illuminated entry. The short options list included the rear spoiler, floor mats and polished wheels.

Additions to the aluminum-block 4.6-liter DOHC V-8 continued unchanged from 1999: a new intake manifold, engine management computer and entire exhaust system from the catalytic converter back. The Cobra produced a true 320 horsepower this year, and enthusiasts ordered 3,867 coupes and 3,384 convertibles.

2001 Cobra Production Chart

Model	Price	Weight	Production
47 (coupe Cobra)	$28,605	3,430	3,867
46 (convertible Cobra)	$32,605	3,560	3,384
Year Total			7,251

2001 Cobra Engine

Code	Engine	Power (hp)	Transmission
V	281-cid (4.6-liter) DOHC V-8	320	M5

2001 SALEEN S-281 SPEEDSTER

2001 SALEEN S-281

The standard 2001 S-281 power plant was the 285-horsepower version of Ford's 4.6-liter V-8 with modified EEC-V strategy, underdrive pulleys, a performance air filter, less-restrictive mufflers and freer-flowing exhaust pipes Saleen had been using since 1999. The S-281 came with Ford's Tremec five-speed or optional four-speed automatic.

S-281 aerodynamic features continued unchanged from 2000, with the exception of the GT's new fake hood scoop, to which Saleen added a unique louvered insert.

The supercharged S/C model met California's strict Transitional Low Emissions Vehicle (TLEV) standards because Ford increased the 4.6-liter's compression ratio from 9.0:1 to 9.4:1. This allowed Saleen to avoid the gas-guzzler tax while retaining the GT's 3.27:1 rear axle gear.

Standard wheels and tires were P255/35ZR18 Pirelli P7000s on 18 x 9-inch wheels in front and P265/35ZR18 Pirellis in back. An upgrade package brought Pirelli's PZeros measuring P265/35ZR18 in front and P295/35ZR18 in the rear for $1,050 each. Most S-281s were shipped in 2001 with the extra-cost chrome wheels.

The S-281 could again be ordered with a Roots-type supercharger with a bypass valve for a more efficient flow of boost resulting in an increase to 365 horsepower. This "Series II" package included all S-281 standard equipment plus the twin-gauge pod (displaying boost and intercooler temperature).

2001 Saleen Production Chart		
Model	**Price**	**Production**
42 (coupe S-281)	$32,099	262
42 (coupe S-281 S/C)	$37,499	243
47 (coupe S-281 Cobra)	$41,600	9
45 (convertible S-281)	$36,099	167
45 (convertible S-281 S/C)	$41,500	223
46 (convertible S-281 Cobra)	$45,500	6
42 (coupe SR)	$158,000	1*
Year Total		911
* Figure includes 1 competition model.		

2001 ROUSH MUSTANG STAGE 3

ROUSH MUSTANG

NASCAR enthusiasts already know Jack Roush from his ownership of Winston Cup Ford teams with Mark Martin, Matt Kenseth and Jeff Burton in the driver's seat. For several decades Roush has had his hands in every aspect of the performance world, including research and development for the Big Three automakers and engine building for motorsports, street, aviation and marine applications.

In 1997 Roush began producing a series of performance packages for V-6 and V-8 Mustangs that could be ordered through Ford dealerships around the country, starting with the least budget-friendly Sport, which can be applied to either V-6 or V-8 Mustangs and includes a complete body kit, side-exit exhaust and the nifty trunk-mounted tool kit but no engine mods.

The next step in the Roush ladder, the Stage 1, expands the Sport theme. Stage 1 makes the rear spoiler standard and includes a set of 17 x 8-inch argent wheels and tires. Stage 2, for GT-based conversions only, adds 18-inch argent wheels and tires plus a lowered performance suspension to the Stage 1 package. The first engine upgrade comes at the Stage 3 level, where the stock 4.6-liter V-8 increases output to 379 horsepower using an Eaton supercharger and computer recalibration. The Stage 3 Sport delivers the more powerful engine combined with an aluminum flywheel, sub-frame connectors, 17-inch argent wheels, Cobra hood and cosmetic package as well as Roush's brake system. The Stage 3 Rally adds a lowered suspension system, 18-inch wheels, racing-style alloy pedals and white-face gauges. All Stage 3 Roush Mustangs receive individual serial numbered-plaques to indicate order and year of production.

For outright go-fast enthusiasts, the 380R features the supercharged engine, Cobra hood, cosmetic upgrades, serial-numbered plaque, Roush brake system and a nostalgic stripe package meant to evoke memories of Carroll Shelby's GT-350s.

For 2003 Roush teamed with legendary hot rod builder and custom wheel designer Boyd Coddington to produce a run of 100 convertibles.

2002 MUSTANG

2002 MUSTANG

Ford's most significant new piece of equipment on the 2002 Mustang was the optional Mach 1000 stereo system, which delivered 1,140 watts of peak power to a 60-watt amplifier, six 85-watt subwoofer amplifiers, four subwoofer speakers, four midrange tweeters and two 10-inch acoustic suspension subwoofer enclosures that consumed most of the trunk space. Audiophiles could also order an MP3-compatible CD player.

The V-6 Mustang received a new 16-inch wheel design finished in bright polished aluminum.

Standard equipment included air conditioning, power windows, power locks, tilt steering column, remote keyless entry, reclining cloth bucket front and — on coupes — a 50/50 fold-down rear seat. Convertibles were equipped with a scratch-resistant glass window and semi-hard boot cover.

Traction control, which had been optional on most models, became standard on the premium V-6 Mustangs and all V-8 cars. Considering the rear-drive Mustang was not designed for maximum traction in slippery conditions, this computer-run system that retards ignition timing and limits fuel flow when it detects wheel spin made the vehicle that much more practical as an everyday ride.

Despite having "only" two airbags, the Mustang was awarded the government's highest rating for crashworthiness in 2002.

2002 Production Chart			
Model	Price	Weight	Production
40 (coupe)	$18,100	3,064	*
40 (dlx coupe)	$18,705	3,066	*
44 (dlx convertible)	$23,625	3,208	*
40 (premium coupe)	$19,820	3,066	*
44 (premium convertible)	$26,210	3,208	*
42 (dlx coupe GT)	$23,845	3,241	*
45 (dlx convertible GT)	$28,100	3,379	*
42 (premium coupe GT)	$25,015	3,241	*
45 (premium convertible GT)	$29,270	3,379	*
Year Total			142,404
* Numbers were unavailable at the time of printing.			

2002 SALEEN S-281

2002 SALEEN S-281

Saleen's S-281 and S-281 S/C models changed very little for 2002. The company made the once-optional composite hood a standard item, which should have eliminated the GT's fake, forward-facing scoop. However, a few '02s were built with the earlier hood. Saleen designer Phil Frank reconfigured the S-281 rear wing, giving it "legs" that ran from the top of the deck lid along the outboard side of the taillights to the body break line, creating the illusion of a wider body. An S-281 badge on the fender replaced the old horse-and-bars emblem.

The base S-281 was once again rated at 285 horsepower, and the S/C featured the same potent 365-hp Series II supercharger option it gained the year before. Both power plants came standard with Ford's Tremec-built five-speed manual transmission.

MaxGrip high-performance differentials were available for $1,395 each in 2002. The MaxGrip operated like a traditional open differential until slippery conditions or applications of torque caused the fluid-type limited slip mechanism to transfer power to the wheel with traction.

Standard wheels and tires on the S-281 and S-281 S/C were P255/35ZR18 Pirelli PZero Neros on 18 x 9-inch wheels in front and P265/35ZR18 Pirellis in back. An upgrade package brought Pirelli's PZero Rossos measuring P265/35ZR18 in front and P295/35ZR18 in the rear to owners for $1,150 each.

The S-281 interior was enhanced with Saleen's traditional white-faced gauges (including a 200-mph speedometer). Six buyers took advantage of the company's offer to apply custom paint for $6,000 each.

2002 Saleen Production Chart		
Model	**Price**	**Production**
42 (coupe S-281)	$34,194	202
42 (coupe S-281 S/C)	$40,299	242
42 (coupe S-281E)	$60,190	34
45 (convertible S-281)	$38,194	138
45 (convertible S-281 S/C)	$44,299	199
45 (convertible S-281E)	$64,089	20
Year Total		835

2002 SALEEN S-281E

2002 SALEEN S-281E

With the end of the scary-fast S-351 in 1999 Saleen Inc. lost its top-of-the-line, premium-priced flagship model, prompting its engineers to create a suitable replacement.

The S-281E — named for Steve Saleen's directive that it be an "extreme-performance Mustang" — featured an engine modified from the block up, with a Saleen-spec forged steel crankshaft, forged steel connecting rods, forged aluminum pistons and E-specific aluminum cylinder heads wearing high-performance valve springs and camshafts. Saleen installed its own version of a 90mm mass airflow sensor, inlet tube and intake manifold, with exhaust routed through a full 2.5-inch stainless steel exhaust system with four-way catalytic converters and an X-configuration crossover pipe.

Saleen engineers went with a Lysholm-built screw compressor supercharger that came to be known as the "Series V." The result was 425 horsepower and 440 lb-ft of torque, which was fed through a standard six-speed manual transmission, 8.8-inch rear axle, 3.08:1 gears and MaxGrip limited-slip differential. E models received Saleen's premium brake package,

with two-piece, slotted front discs measuring 13 inches clamped by four-piston calipers. Rolling stock was made up of Pirelli's PZero Rossos (P265/35ZR18 in front, P295/35ZR18 in rear) on 18 x 9- and 18 x 10-inch five-spoke alloy wheels.

The S-281E received the base model's bodywork with the exception of a special louvered hood and a rear wing from the retired S-351. A center-exit dual exhaust system and matching rear valance were standard on the E and not available on the regular S-281 models.

At $60,190 for the coupe and $64,089 for the convertible, it is understandable there were virtually no options save for chrome wheels, Speedster package and custom paint.

2002 Saleen Engines			
Code	Engine	Power (hp)	Transmission
X	281-cid (4.6-liter) V-8 SOHC	285	M5, A4
X	281-cid (4.6-liter) V-8 SOHC super	365	M5, A4
X	281-cid (4.6-liter) V-8 SOHC E super	425	M6

SALEEN CENTER EXHAUST

SALEEN CENTER EXHAUST

Some of Saleen's advertisements featuring the re-designed 1999 S-281 and S-351 models show a pair of exhaust tips exiting the rear bumper side-by-side in the center of the panel. The company intended to install this exotic bit of plumbing on every S-351 built that year. The feature was also scheduled for the S-281 options list.

Unfortunately, the Environmental Protection Agency would not allow Saleen to use the center exhaust outlets because it placed hot pipes directly beneath the S-351's stock gas tank, where the heat would greatly increase the car's evaporative emissions.

The twin center pipes would not see the light of day again until 2002, when they became standard equipment on the new S-281E model and an extra-cost option on the rest of the Saleen Mustang line.

2003 MUSTANG GT LIMITED EDITION

2003 MUSTANG

In 2003 the Mustang was entirely alone in the marketplace, a niche it had created nearly four decades earlier, when General Motors ended production of Chevrolet's Camaro and Pontiac's Firebird.

The base Mustang continued with its 3.8-liter overhead valve V-6 engine putting out 190 horsepower. Available as a well-appointed model for the budget-minded, the coupe and convertible could be enhanced with a deluxe package that added a rear spoiler, floor mats, power driver's seat and cruise control or a premium group that included a leather-wrapped steering wheel, Mach 460 stereo, ABS, traction control and a lower body stripe. V-6 owners could also take advantage of a Pony package that upgraded

the car's appearance with a GT hood, 16-inch polished aluminum wheels, "stampede" graphics and a leather-wrapped steering wheel.

In its advertising Ford touted several safety improvements for the '03 Mustang, such as a new design for the A-pillar, headliner and sun visors.

2002 Engines				
Code	Engine	Intake	Power (hp)	Transmission
4	232-cid V-6	EFI	190	M5, A4
R	281-cid V-8 DOHC Mach 1	EFI	305	M5, A4
X	281-cid V-8 SOHC	EFI	260	M5, A4
Y	281-cid V-8 DOHC Cobra Super	EFI	390	M6

2003 MUSTANG MACH 1

2003 MACH 1

The 1969 to '73 Mach 1 was certainly the most popular performance package available on the early Mustang. More than 72,000 were sold during its introductory year. A range of high-performance engines was available to power the SportsRoof-only model down the quarter-mile or long stretch of highway, including several 351s, a few 428s and ultimately a 429 in Super Cobra Jet trim.

The Mach 1 name carried over to the Mustang II generation, where its reputation suffered from the absence of a legitimate power plant.

Ford's product planners saw a gap in 2003 between the base Mustang V-8 GT and the more expensive SVT Cobra. Ford filled that gap with a retro version of the Mach 1 designed by the same folks responsible for the '01 Bullitt. The new Mach 1 featured a "Shaker" intake scoop that stood above the surface of the hood and fed air to a 305-horsepower DOHC 4.6-liter V-8. The modern version's shaking was the result of clever spring and vacuum hose work.

The new Mach 1 could be shifted with either the standard five-speed or four-speed automatic. Both transmissions fed their power through a 3.55:1 rear axle. Suspension enhancements brought the car down a half-inch closer to the ground and 13-inch Brembo brakes (front) and 11.7-inch Brembo discs (rear) made the car stop as quickly as it went. To ensure that only the hood scoop shook while accelerating, engineers installed subframe connectors on the torquey Mach 1's chassis.

Other features included a Mach 1-specific chin spoiler, a tape stripe running from the leading edge of the hood to the cowl vent and a black free-standing rear wing as well as a set of 17-inch five-spoke alloy wheels that strongly resembled the original's Magnum 500. The driver's environment was modified to reflect a late-'60s style.

When Ford announced the late-2003 availability of the Mach 1 package, only 6,500 units were planned.

By the end of the model year 9,652 Mach 1s had been sold.

2003 SVT COBRA

2003 SVT COBRA

SVT delayed development of its next-generation Mustang-based super car and skipped the 2002 model year. Anxious Mustang fans were aware the company was planning a Cobra more powerful than any Mustang ever made—including the Boss 429s and Super Cobra Jets of the 1960s. When it was released, the 2003 Cobra not only met the high standards set by those tire-shredding muscle cars; it easily surpassed them.

With its supercharged 4.6-liter double overhead cam engine, the new SVT Cobra's output rated at 390 hp and 390 lb-ft of torque. Eaton's Roots-type supercharger was tuned to produce eight pounds of boost and a water-to-air intercooler reduced the temperature of the charge for maximum combustion mixture volatility. To strengthen the powertrain against such violent internal forces, the new Cobra engine was built from a cast-iron block. A six-speed Tremec T-56 manual was the only transmission available. An accelerator-friendly 3.55:1 rear axle backed it up.

With driver and passenger airbags, anti-lock braking on four-wheel discs, traction control and independent rear suspension all standard equipment, the new Cobra was also safer and better handling than its legendary predecessors.

SVT released its 10th Anniversary Edition SVT Cobra later that summer, available in either coupe or convertible body styles. Only 2,003 of the anniversary Cobras — to be painted red, black or silver — were produced.

In all, SVT produced 8,394 2003 Cobra coupes and 5,082 Cobra convertibles.

2003 Cobra Production Chart			
Model	Price	Weight	Production
48 (coupe Cobra)	$34,065	3,665	8,394
49 (convertible Cobra)	$38,405	3,780	5,082
Year Total			13,476

2003 Cobra Engines			
Code	Engine	Power (hp)	Transmission
Y	281-cid (4.6-liter) DOHC V-8	390	M6

2003 SALEEN S-281

2003 SALEEN S-281

All of Saleen's S-281 models enjoyed power increases for 2003, starting with a jump to 290 horsepower for the base car due to a new high-flow exhaust system with 2.5-inch diameter pipes and a reconfigured engine management computer. Carried over from 2002 were the performance air filter, underdrive pulleys and less-restrictive mufflers. The S-281 came standard with a Tremec five-speed or optional four-speed automatic transmission — both with a standard 3.27:1 rear axle.

The stock GT hood—wearing a Saleen-designed scoop and louvered insert—returned to the base S-281 unless the expensive composite unit was specified.

The S/C's rating increased to 375 horsepower by way of a new Lysholm screw-type supercharger (known as the "Series IV") similar to the compressor introduced on the 2002 E. The standard rear axle with the S/C package had 3.55:1 gearing.

The E model was boosted to 445 horsepower when engineers switched to a larger throttle body and smaller supercharger pulley. The Lysholm blower continued to pump out 12 pounds of boost, which was handled by the E's standard six-speed manual transmission, 8.8-inch rear axle, 3.55:1 gears and MaxGrip limited-slip differential. An improved brake package was standard, with two-piece, slotted front discs measuring 14 inches clamped by four-piston calipers.

2003 Saleen Production Chart		
Model	**Price**	**Production**
42 (coupe S-281)	$36,095	84
42 (coupe S-281 S/C)	$42,788	128
48 (coupe S-281 Cobra)	$47,664	6
42 (coupe S-281E)	$60,190	4
45 (convertible S-281)	$40,114	53
45 (convertible S-281 S/C)	$46,807	100
49 (convertible S-281 Cobra)	$51,698	5
45 (convertible S-281E)	$64,089	10
45 (convertible SA-20)	$54,257	10
45 (convertible S-281)	$66,410	2*
Year Total		402

2003 SALEEN SA-20

2003 SALEEN SA-20

Wearing traditional company colors of yellow, black and white in 2003, Saleen Inc.'s S-281 SA-20 model commemorated the California firm's 20-year history of high-performance Mustang production. Some combination of these hues dressed every one of the Saleen anniversary cars, including the SA-10 (1993) and SA-15 ('98).

Motivated by a 375 horsepower S/C powertrain and wearing a convertible body, the SA-20 package added the S-281E's rear wing, plus anniversary-specific equipment such as a Speedster tonneau cover (with integrated light bar), custom painted pearl white 18 x 9-inch wheels, SA-20 graphics and ID, console plaque, door panels, floor mats and key fob.

Saleen's marketers turned the SA-20 into a sales success by building a whole experience around its purchase. The $54,357 price (including a $10,000 non-refundable deposit) covered airfare for two to Irvine, one night's lodging, a celebratory dinner with Steve Saleen and attendance at the facility's seventh annual car show.

Brake upgrades were the most popular SA-20 extra-cost equipment, with five of the six cars receiving 13-inch front discs and one being built with 14-inchers. All six buyers ponied up for the 18 x 10-inch rear wheel option; five ordered Performance Cooling. Only one was built with Ford's automatic transmission.

2003 Saleen Engines			
Code	Engine	Power (hp)	Transmission
X	281-cid (4.6-liter) V-8 SOHC	290	M5, A4
X	281-cid (4.6-liter) V-8 SOHC super	375	M5, A4
Y	281-cid (4.6-liter) V-8 DOHC Cobra super	390	M6
X	281-cid (4.6-liter) V-8 SOHC E super	445	M6

2004 MUSTANG

2004 MUSTANG

Ford's early photos of an incredibly beautiful 2005 Mustang replacement sent America into a "next generation" frenzy and slowed sales for the long-in-the-tooth 2004 model. Things stayed the same mechanically for 2004 — the final year of the SN-95 platform Ford introduced as a 1994 model — leaving a couple of new paint options, a commemorative badge and an anniversary package to attract customers.

All Mustangs were improved for 2004 with stiffer accessory drive brackets and more refined bearings.

In its second year, the Mach 1 package did not change, although the 4.6-liter DOHC engine was given a slightly different rating than what had been advertised in 2003. Automatic transmission-equipped Mach 1s were rated at 308 horsepower at 5,800 rpm. Those shifting through a five-speed were rewarded with 310 at 6,000.

2004 Engines				
Code	Engine	Intake	Power (hp)	Transmission
4	232-cid V-6	EFI	190	M5, A4
R	281-cid V-8 DOHC Mach 1	EFI	310	M5
R	281-cid V-8 DOHC Mach 1	EFI	308	A4
X	281-cid V-8 SOHC	EFI	260	M5, A4
Y	281-cid V-8 DOHC Cobra Super	EFI	390	M6

2004 MUSTANG 40TH ANNIVERSARY BADGE

MUSTANG 40TH ANNIVERSARY BADGE AND MODEL

Ford applied a special fender badge to all 2004 Mustangs to commemorate the line's 40th anniversary, and a cosmetic enhancement package was available to mark the milestone as well.

Offered exclusively in Crimson Red as well as Black or Oxford White on either the V-6 or GT platform, the 40th Anniversary Mustangs received Arizona Beige Metallic performance stripes on the hood, lower rocker panels and deck lid plus upgraded wheels. Anniversary cars were fitted with deluxe Medium Parchment interiors featuring four-way head restraints, painted center console surrounds, metallic gray shifter bezel and door lock knobs, shift boot trim and pedals finished in brushed aluminum.

2004 SVT COBRA

2004 SVT COBRA

In 2004 everyone on the planet was eagerly awaiting the all-new Mustang design promised by Ford for 2005, so SVT carried its 390-horse-power coupes and convertibles into a second year without any major changes.

In addition to a color-shifting Mystichrome appearance package, SVT offered two more traditional colors for its Cobras: Screaming Yellow and Competition Orange. Otherwise, the only options available were chromed wheels and a rear spoiler delete.

The exhaust system was slightly updated, which helped to eliminate the Gas Guzzler Tax that the 2003 suffered. There were also some minor interior changes.

2004 Cobra Production Chart

Model	Price	Weight	Production
48 (coupe Cobra)	$35,370	3,665	3,768
49 (convertible Cobra)	$39,750	3,780	1,896
Year Total			5,664

2004 Cobra Engine

Code	Engine	Power (hp)	Transmission
Y	281-cid (4.6-liter) DOHC V-8	390	M6

2004 SALEEN S-281

2004 SALEEN S-281

There were no major changes to Saleen's S-281-based models for 2004, primarily due to Ford's upcoming all-new Mustang platform scheduled for a 2005 introduction.

With an advertised 290 horsepower, the base S-281 was the most affordable of the series and could be ordered with a five-speed manual or four-speed automatic and standard 3.27:1 or optional 3.55:1 rear axle gears. Buyers could pay extra to have their S-281s fitted with the E-style wing, which was essentially the old S-351 piece.

The S-281 S/C received a screw-type supercharger compressor to pump out an advertised 375 horsepower through a five-speed manual and 3.55:1 standard rear axle. The E-style rear wing was standard on the S/C for 2004, along with a center exhaust system and appropriate rear valance panel.

Saleen-modified SVT Cobras continued to trickle from the Irvine plant, just as they had since the S-281's introduction in 1996, even though the company never advertised their availability. The Cobra DOHC engine was left untouched, but Saleen installed its suspension, interior, cosmetic and aerodynamic equipment on each car. For 2003 and 2004, the 390-horsepower Cobra model fit squarely (in terms of price and performance) between Saleen's S/C and the E model.

The E continued as the company's flagship model in its third year with no changes.

2004 Saleen Production Chart		
Model	**Price**	**Production**
42 (coupe S-281)	$36,629	*
42 (coupe S-281 S/C)	$43,322	*
48 (coupe S-281 Cobra)	N/A	*
42 (coupe S-281E)	$61,120	*
45 (convertible S-281)	$40,688	*
45 (convertible S-281 S/C)	$47,381	*
49 (convertible S-281 Cobra)	N/A	*
45 (convertible S-281E)	$65,078	*
45 (convertible S-281)	N/A	**
Year Total	*	
* Production figures not available at time of printing. ** Canadian-built Saleens		

2005 MUSTANG GT

2005 MUSTANG

The 2005 Mustang was arguably the most successful "retro" car on the market from a design standpoint. It represented a smooth blend of 1969 Mach 1, 1966 Shelby GT-350 and early GT style points. Even the famous "spinner" hubcap made a return of sorts on the base model.

Designers wisely retained the Mustang's traditional long hood/short deck profile. Subtle C-shaped indentions mimic the 1965 model's sculpted sides, a galloping horse stands out against the black background of the grille, and the taillamps are each made up of three vertical elements.

The "S197"— its insider name — was slight-ly larger in every dimension than the SN-95 it replaced, including overall length (187.6 vs. 183.2 for the '04), width (73.9 vs. 73.1), height (54.5 vs. 53.1), wheelbase (107.1 vs. 101.3), front/rear track (62.8/63 vs. 59.9/60.1) and fuel capacity (16 gallons vs. 15.7). The V-6 model with the five-speed manual transmission only gained 10 pounds over the 2004 (3,300 up from 3,290), but the manual-shift GT put on 103 pounds (to 3,450).

Passenger dimensions improved by a half-inch to a full inch all around (with an overall cabin improvement from 83 cubic feet to 98), and cargo capacity went from 10.9 cubic feet in 2004 to 13.0 for 2005.

2005 Production Chart

Model	Price	Weight	Production
110A (deluxe coupe)	$19,410	3,351	*
120A (premium coupe)	$19,995	3,351	*
130A GT (deluxe coupe)	$24,995	3,483	*
140A GT (premium coupe)	$26,330	3,483	*
Year Total			*
* Numbers were unavailable at the time of printing.			

2005 Engines

Code	Engine	Intake	Power (hp)	Transmission
N	245-cid V-6 SOHC	SFI	210	M5, A5
H	281-cid V-8 SOHC	SFI	300	M5, A5

2005 MUSTANG

2005 MUSTANG MODELS

Only four Mustang models were offered at the start of the 2005 selling season: a Deluxe and Premium V-6 coupe and a Deluxe and Premium GT coupe. As has been the case in past introductory periods, the convertible was released a few months later in the spring.

The base Mustang, the V-6 Deluxe, came standard with four-wheel power disc brakes, the 245-cid (4.0-liter) SOHC V-6, Tremec T-5 five-speed manual transmission, remote keyless entry, rear window defroster, stainless steel single exhaust, dual power side mirrors, 16 x 7-inch painted cast aluminum wheels, P215/65R16 blackwall Goodrich tires, air conditioning, AM/FM stereo with single CD player, center console, front floor mats, door map pockets, cloth front bucket seats with 50/50 split rear bench in the coupe, tilt steering wheel, speed control, power windows and door locks and dual front air bags.

To this list the V-6 Premium package added 16-inch bright machines aluminum wheels with chrome spinner, Shaker 500 audio system with six-disc CD changer and MP3 capability, six-way

power adjustable driver seat and leather seats.

Moving up to the GT Deluxe continued the upgrades with the 281-cid (4.6-liter) three-valve SOHC V-8 engine, ABS with traction control, stainless steel dual exhaust, fog lamps, complex reflector halogen headlights with integral turn signals, rear spoiler, 17 x 8-inch painted cast aluminum wheels with P235/55ZR17 high-performance Pirelli tires, AM/FM stereo with single CD and cloth sport bucket seats.

The top-of-the-line GT Premium model added a Shaker 500 audio system with six-disc CD player and leather-trimmed sport bucket seats.

An Interior Upgrade Package (optional on all models) brought with it the bright instrument cluster with adjustable colors, leather shift knob, satin-aluminum steering wheel spokes, satin door handles and scuff plates, message center and leather-wrapped steering wheel. The Interior Color Accent Package (also available on all models with Interior Upgrade Package) included red leather seating surfaces and red door inserts and red floor mats.

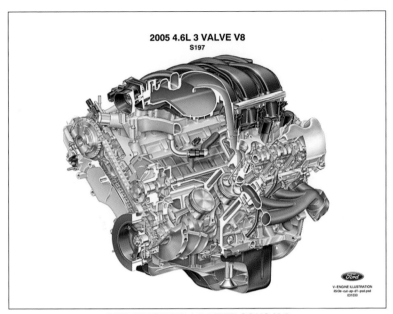

2005 MUSTANG 4.6-LITER SOHC V-8

2005 MUSTANG POWERTRAINS

2005 was a real leap forward for Mustang powertrain technology, with a lot of "firsts" and "mosts" sitting under the long aluminum hoods of the base and GT models.

The base 2005 brought the first V-6 to the Mustang line with single overhead camshafts, which helped it achieve a respectable 210 horsepower at 5,250 rpm with a suggested redline of 6,100 rpm. Realize that rating makes the 60-degree 4.0-liter V-6 as strong as or stronger than the heavier 1982 through 1986 5.0-liter V-8s in terms of horsepower. Hooked to the V-6 was a standard Tremec T-5 five-speed manual transmission or optional, first-ever, five-speed automatic transmission.

The 300-horsepower 4.6-liter V-8 was the most powerful engine installed in a modern Mustang GT, built from an aluminum block and heads (a first for the GT) and topped off with three valves per cylinder (two intake, one exhaust — another first), magnesium cam covers, single overhead camshafts and variable valve timing. Manual shifting was handled by a Tremec 3650 five-speed and the same 5R55S automatic five-speed offered with the V-6 engine was an extra-cost option.

Mustangs with V-8 engines received 8.8-inch rear axles. GTs with manual transmissions were fitted with 3.55:1 rear axle gears; all other models had 3.31:1 cogs installed.

2005 SALEEN S-281

2005 SALEEN S-281

The new S179 Mustang design sent Saleen and its competitors back to their CAD/CAM programs. Saleen chose to mimic its own successful S7 super car, giving the S-281 similar styling cues in the aerodynamics package. This family resemblance was especially strong in the taillight panel, wing and rear valance.

The new S-281 appeared longer in profile than Ford's Mustang because it was, thanks to an extended tail section that recessed the 1960s-style taillamps and blacked-out panel in between. Subtle design flourishes included a flat rear wing, triangular quarter-window inserts, absent foglamps, hungry-looking front spoiler and functional hood vents.

Saleen once again leapfrogged Ford in wheel diameter, this time by a whole three inches! The stock Mustang GT wheels were 17s, which Saleen replaced with 20-inch alloys (again reminiscent of those found on the S7) wrapped with Pirelli PZero Rosso ultra-performance radials.

Horsepower ratings were advertised as 325 for the base S-281 (up from Ford's 300), 400 for the supercharged S/C model, and an anticipated 500 for the late-release S-281E car. All engines were based on Ford's three-valve 4.6-liter V-8. An optional 14-inch front brake package worked in concert with Saleen's standard traditional Racecraft suspension components to produce braking and handling on par with Chevy's more expensive Corvette.

Pricing for the 2005 base Saleen S-281 started at around $39,043 and $46,134 for the supercharged model.

2005 Saleen Engines			
Code	Engine	Power (hp)	Transmission
H	281-cid V-8 SOHC	325	M5, A5
H	281-cid V-8 SOHC super	400	M5, A5
H	281-cid V-8 SOHC E super	500	M6

2005½ MUSTANG CONVERTIBLE

2005½ MUSTANG CONVERTIBLE

The "drop-top" version of the new generation 2005 Mustang was introduced to the public on Super Bowl Sunday, February 6, 2005, in a television ad that showed a state trooper pulling up behind a Mustang convertible driver at an intersection that resembled Saskatchewan or Siberia.

The officer attempted to talk to the driver, only to find he was frozen in place with the top down and a smile on his face. The tag in the ad mentions that winter is not the time to bring out the Mustang convertible so Ford is waiting until spring.

In its auto show materials, Ford promised that "...thanks to intelligent engineering that resulted in a convertible platform with more than twice the torsional stiffness of the previous version, this is the most quiet and solid drop top Mustang ever produced. The squeaks, shakes and rattles to which cars without fixed metal roofs typically are prone are startlingly missing from the 2005 Mustang convertible."

The Mustang convertible features a glass rear window with defroster, full quarter windows and a raked windshield that blocks the wind from front seat passengers.

The pre-engineering of the convertible promises a rigid structure without a great deal of added weight and promises a ride that is similar to the coupe.

Other features of the 2005½ Mustang convertible include power-assisted rack-and-pinion steering, disk brakes all around and four channel ABS on the Mustang GT convertible. Standard tires on the GT are W-rated P235/55R-17 all season performance radials riding on 17-inch rims. The V-6 version has 16 x 7- inch wheels with T-rated P215/65R-16 all season radial tires.

The Mustang convertible is powered by a standard 4.0-liter 210 hp SOHC V-6 while the GT version has the same 300 hp 4.6-liter V-8 as the GT coupe. The Tremec five-speed manual transmission comes standard.

2005½ Mustang Convertible Engines		
Engine	Power (hp)	Transmission
4.0 liter SOHC V-6	210	M5, A5
4.6 liter SOHC V-8	300	M5, A5

2007 MUSTANG

2007 MUSTANG

Now in its third model year showcasing the retro reincarnation of the late-1960s styling cues, the 2007 Mustang lineup added a few performance models (Shelby GT500 and GT California Special models are profiled elsewhere) to its regular line. The 2007s were also offered again in both fastback and convertible formats in both base and GT models, and there were again Deluxe andPremium categories of trim in each model.

New for 2007 were heated front seats, optional on both base and GT models. Added to the standard component list was a digital audio jack. The Pony Package returned for base Premium models and again included GT-style grille-mounted foglamps, rear spoiler and 17-inch wheels.

Base models were again propelled by the overhead-cam, two-valves-per-cylinder 4.0-liter, 210-hp V-6 with a 9.7 compression ratio.

GT models used the overhead-cam, three-valves-per-cylinder 4.6-liter, 300-hp V-8 with a 9.8 compression ratio. Five-speed manual or five-speed automatic were again the transmission choices.

Key features in 2007 basically mirrored '06. Base Deluxe standard equipment included dual front airbags, four-wheel disc brakes, cruise control, remote keyless entry, theft-deterrent system and alloy wheels.

Moving up to the base Premium trim level added a six-way power driver's seat with lumbar adjustment and an upgraded audio system.

The GT Deluxe package added traction control, a limited-slip differential, anti-lock four-wheel disc brakes, leather-wrapped steering wheel, rear spoiler and foglamps. Going Premium on the GT models included leather uphostery and a further upgraded audio system from base Premium's audio offering.

2008 BULLITT MUSTANG

2008 MUSTANG BULLITT EDITION

On the 40th anniversary of the release of the Steve McQueen movie "Bullitt," Ford debuted its 2008 Mustang Bullitt fastback. Ford engineers went so far as to create a unique H-pipe dual exhaust system for the car to mimic the sound of Frank Bullitt's (McQueen's character's name) 390-cid-V-8-powered 1968 movie Mustang.

The 2008 Bullitt was certainly a different beast than the 2001 Mustang Bullitt Edition — that earlier-generation production car was the result of a wildly successful concept car shown at the 2000 Los Angeles Auto Show. The 2008 Mustang Bullitt fastback, with its retro-'60s styling cues, was a truer representation of the original movie car.

Another of Ford's annual "Steed For Every Need" feature Mustangs, the latest Bullitt was a limited edition with a production of 7,700 units spread over two model years (5,600 in '08 and 2,100 in '09). It could be ordered in either black or, for the purists, original-to-the-movie-version Dark Highland Green.

The 2008 Bullitt Edition Mustang was powered by a 4.6-liter V-8 that produced 315 hp and 325 lbs.-ft. of torque. It featured a new-for-2008 adaptive spark ignition system that offered on-the-fly spark adjustment to provide maximum torque. The engine was calibrated to increase throttle response and offered a top speed of 150 mph and a redline of 6,500 rpm. The V-8 was mated to a Tremec five-speed manual transmission with a Bullitt-unique polished aluminum ball on the shifter for enhanced grip.

Outside, in tribute to the badge-free original '68 movie car (including a "ponyless" grille), the lone identification of the 2008 version was a "Bullitt" graphic inscribed on the decklid's faux gas cap. Also, the car employed unique cast-aluminum Euroflange wheels, and their Dark Argent Gray spokes featured a satin finish. Brake calipers were colored to match the wheels.

Internally, the Bullitt was "clean" and designed to mimic the bare exterior. Charcoal black leather seats and Satin metallic trim were complemented by a hand-machined, aluminum-swirl dash panel applique. The foot pedals also sported aluminum covers to enhance the car's performance heritage.

2008 MUSTANG

2008 MUSTANG

After finding unparalleled sales success, Ford returned with the 2008 Mustang lineup intact from the previous year. The few changes included three additional exterior colors, side-impact air bags added as standard equipment and new available features such as High Intensity Discharge (HID) headlamps, 18-inch wheels on the V-6 fastback and an interior ambient lighting system that allowed front occupants to select from seven different hues to illuminate footwells and cupholders. Also, recalling the days of FoMoCo's founder Henry Ford and his penchant for allowing nothing to go to waste and finding less expensive ways to produce automobiles, Ford began utilizing soybeans in the seating material of all 2008 Mustangs.

Additionally, Ford offered Mustang buyers a limited-edition "Warriors in Pink" model that was designed exclusively in support of the 25th anniversary Susan G. Komen for the Cure breast cancer research foundation. The Warriors in Pink Mustangs featured a pink ribbon and pony fender badge, pink Mustang rocker tape stripe, charcoal leather seats with pink stitching, leather-wrapped aluminum-spoke steering wheel with pink stitching and a unique pony grille with chrome bezel and fog lamps.

Also, in 2008, a convertible version of the Shelby GT-H (Hertz) Mustang joined the rental car company's "Rent-A-Racer" fleet that originated in 2006 with a fastback-only offering as part of Hertz's Fun Collection. Production of 500 of these rental ragtops was carried out at Carroll Shelby's Shelby Automobiles in Las Vegas.

2008 SHELBY GT500KR

2008 MUSTANG SHELBY GT500KR

It was hailed as the most powerful production Mustang ever built. On the 40th anniversary of the launch of the original "KR" (King of the Road), Ford unleashed the 2008 Shelby GT500KR fastback in what it termed a 1,000-build, limited-edition model. The car was a collaboration of Ford Racing, Ford SVT (Special Vehicle Team) and legendary car builder Carroll Shelby.

The 1968 Shelby Cobra GT500KR was a mid-year launch, and was based on its counterpart GT500. Ford's inclusion of the name Cobra reflected its then-new Cobra Jet 428-cid/335-horsepower V-8 found under the unique fiberglass hood of the original KR. In truth, the KR's advertised horsepower was quite shy of its 400-horse reality. That pioneering KR sold 1,570 units, 1,053 fastbacks and 517 convertibles.

Under its unique dual-scooped, carbon-composite hood, the 2008 GT500KR featured a Ford SVT supercharged 5.4-liter V-8 enhanced with a Ford Racing Power Upgrade Pack. The engine was rated at a hair-raising 540 hp and 510 lbs.-ft. of torque. Power to the ground was delivered via a "short-throw" shifter mounted on top of a Tremec TR6060 six-speed manual transmission and 3.73:1 rear axle ratio.

The KR also featured unique spring rates, dampers and stabilizer bars in its handling package. Externally, the 2008 KR sported stainless-steel twist-lock hood pins, a lower front air dam with chrome-trimmed brake ducting and 14-inch Brembo front brakes. It's specific 40th Anniversary badging on fenders and grille was complemented by unique side and center striping. Inside, the KR had Carroll Shelby-signature embroidered headrests and a 40th Anniversary numbered dash plaque.

And just as the '68 KR made its debut at the 1967 New York Auto Show, the 2008 KR was unveiled at the 2007 New York International Auto Show.

2009 MUSTANG

2009 MUSTANG

In its final year before a 2010 redesign, the big news for Mustang enthusiasts was the 2009 version's option list included a $1,995 glass sunroof. Again offered in fastback and convertible body styles, base and GT models and Deluxe and Premium trim levels, the 2009 Mustang retained powertrains and most everything else offered the previous year.

What did change was the base V-6 and GT V-8 Premium trim level models added an upgraded interior, ambient interior lighting and satellite radio as standard fare.

All in all, the 2009 Mustang offered performance enthusiasts as much bang for their buck as any hot car on the market. Sure, it was still a bit of a gas hog, but the Mustang again compensated with its killer looks, great personality and friendly sticker price.

The Bullitt Edition Mustang, introduced in 2008, the Warriors in Pink Edition Mustang to support the Susan G. Komen Foundation for breast cancer research and the GT-based California Special were again offered in 2009.

2010 SHELBY COBRA GT500

2010 SHELBY COBRA GT500

The venomous snake was back in the Mustang lineup for 2010. While Mustang's Shelby GT500 model was launched in 2007, a newly titled Shelby Cobra GT500 debuted in 2010, again offered in both fastback and convertible versions.

Just about every aspect of the 2010 Cobra GT500 was upgraded when compared to the 2007 model. For starters, power was supplied by what to date was the most powerful Special Vehicle Team (SVT) tuned engine in the form of a supercharged and intercooled 5.4-liter V-8 rated at 540 horsepower and 510 pound-feet of torque. It was mated to a six-speed manual transmission that featured a twin-disc clutch and revised fifth and sixth gearing to improve fuel economy while highway cruising. To offset the more potent go factor, the Cobra GT500 featured improved stopping performance via larger (250mm vs. the previous 215mm) brake discs that were created from fiberglass and copper for added strength and cooling capabilities.

Borrowing from the GT500KR (King of the Road) model's suspension, the Cobra GT500 received enhanced chassis tuning, with a greater emphasis placed on primary body control. The car's steering shaft was stiffened and springs and dampers were calibrated for better roll control. The fastback now rode on 19-inch forged aluminum wheels and the convertible on 18-inchers.

The exterior was revised with the addition of a more aggressive appearing front splitter and an integrated Gurney Flap on the rear spoiler. Cobra badging moved to a new location on the grille and was also present on front fenders. Racing stripes were newly available on the convertible and again offered on the fastback.

Inside, the Cobra GT500 used real leather in its seating and real aluminum on the instrument panel. The panel featured a three-dimensional dimpled-texture pattern inspired by racing clutch plates.

2010 MUSTANG

2010 FORD MUSTANG

Coincidence? Not likely. With retro-look versions of both the Chevrolet Camaro and Dodge Challenger returning to the marketplace, the Ford Mustang received sweeping changes for the 2010 model year to compete with its rival manufacturers' offerings in the muscle car category.

While the Mustang retained its retro look that was launched in 2005, its overall presentation was tweaked inside and out. What remained the same was that Mustang was again assembled at the Auto Alliance International Plant in Flat Rock, Mich., was solid rear axle driven and still offered in fastback and convertible body styles.

For 2010, the Mustang V-6 and GT V-8 versions could both be ordered in either base or Premium trim levels. Up front, a more forward-swept grille carried a new-look Mustang badge (its first redesign since 1964). Headlamps and turn indicators were integrated into one unit. The V-6's fog lamps were relocated to the lower fascia, while the GT V-8's remained in the grille but were smaller than the 2009 version. Front fenders were also smoother than the previous year, and it was all capped by a powerdome hood that appeared more muscular and allowed for enhanced air cooling of the engine.

Wheel flares for both front and rear became more sculptured than previous editions. Moving to the rear, the Mustang's taillamps were restyled and used LEDs that illuminate progressively when the turn signal was activated. Under the hood, the Mustang V-6 remained at 4.0 liters, but the GT's V-8, due to a revised cold-air induction system, had its horsepower increased from the previous 300 to 315. The five-speed manual transmission was again standard and the five-speed automatic the option.

The Mustang's interior for 2010 was also refined, and now featured a one-piece instrument panel crafted from seamless Thermoplastic Olefin "soft-touch" material. Optional was Ford's new navigation system that utilized a touchscreen command format. Also, Mustang buyers could now customize their ambient and instrument lighting from 125 different color options.

Wheel size also increased one inch across the board, with the V-6 Mustang now riding on 17-inch aluminum wheels with 18-inchers optional while the GT used 18-inch aluminum wheels with 19-inchers the option. AdvanceTrac Electronic Stability Control became standard equipment in 2010 and aided the Mustang's all-speed traction control and anti-lock braking.

2011 SHELBY GT350

2011 MUSTANG SHELBY GT350

With 2005-2010 Mustang variants such as the Shelby GT500/GT500KR (King of the Road)/GT500 Cobra, Bullitt, Shelby GT-H (Hertz) and California Special, it was inevitable that the Shelby GT350 would eventually join the ranks of Mustang muscle. Ford Motor Co., in collaboration with Shelby American in Las Vegas, again returned to its roots via the make-over of the 2011 Ford Mustang GT fastback into a Shelby GT350 — just in time to observe the car's 45th anniversary.

For $33,995 over the cost of a 2011 Mustang GT, Shelby American transformed the fastback into a tribute to that original 1965 Shelby Mustang GT350. Only 522 '65 fastbacks were produced by Carroll Shelby, and those that remain are in high demand among vintage car collectors.

To create the reborn GT350, Shelby American began with an all-white 2011 Mustang GT

fastback. The appearance of the car was via major body modifications to the entire exterior of the car and the addition of Guardsman Blue striping. Exclusive badging included GT350 signature on the grille and 45th anniversary on the rear fascia.

Power for the GT350 came from Ford's 5.0-liter V-8 that was massaged with a Whipple supercharger and topped with monogrammed GT350 valve covers. The GT350 also received Ford Racing's suspension package with a caster/camber plate kit, Baer six-piston front brake kit and enhanced rear brake rotors with front and rear brake ducting and cooling kit, Boria center exit exhaust and 19-inch alloy wheels. Options included the Baer six-piston rear brake kit upgrade, Watts link rear suspension, a Goodyear street/race tire package and a Shelby high-performance cooling system.

2011 MUSTANG

2011 FORD MUSTANG

When conversing about performance cars, a big-block V-8 example usually gets the most attention. Not so for Ford Mustang's 2011 line-up. A new V-6 garnered most of the buzz, even trumping a new V-8. And this V-6 did it with a combination of horsepower and fuel economy, the reflection of new-age demand for old-world performance coupled with "green" mentality fuel savings.

The engine in the limelight was the all-aluminum Duratec 3.7-liter V-6 rated at 305 hp while delivering 30 mpg when equipped with Ford's optional six-speed automatic transmission. A six-speed manual transmission was standard. The dual-overhead cam, 24-valve engine with 10.5:1 compression ratio featured Twin Independent Variable Camshaft Timing (Ti-VCT) that was capable of adjusting the valvetrain in microseconds. This engine was available in the Mustang fastback and convertible, each offered in base or Premium trim levels.

Another reason the Mustang V-6 received attention was its optional Performance Package. Catered to driving enthusiasts, this package consisted of a 3.31 rear axle ratio for better snap off the line, the firmer Mustang GT-level suspension, 19-inch wheels, softer tire compound and an additional strut tower brace for enhanced chassis rigidity.

Also offered in fastback and convertible and in base or Premium trim levels was the Mustang GT. It, too, received a new engine in the form of a dual-overhead cam, 32-valve 5.0-liter V-8 with a 11.0:1 compression ratio and that pumped out 402 hp (on regular fuel or 412 if premium fuel was used). This V-8 also utilized Ti-VTC and could be coupled to the standard six-speed manual transmission or optional six-speed automatic.

Significant changes to the 2011 Mustang lineup from the previous year included the switch to electric (from hydraulic) power steering, larger brakes, revised suspension tuning added noise insulation, blind-spot mirrors and the introduction of Ford's MyKey system that allows for owners to set up driving restrictions for young drivers.

Optional packages for Mustangs continued with both the Pony Package and California Special edition as well as a Mustang Club of America Special Edition.

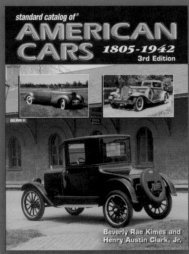
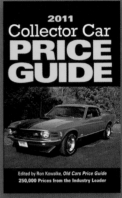

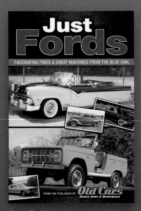

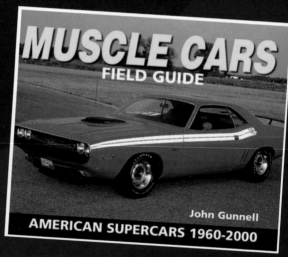